THE RISE AND FALL

OF THE

WELL-MADE PLAY

By the same author

Anatomy for a Television Play

The Angry Theater: New British Drama
(Published in England as *Anger and After*)

Cinema Eye, Cinema Ear: Some Key Film-Makers of the Sixties

The Art Nouveau Book in Britain

John Russell Taylor

THE RISE AND FALL

OF THE

WELL-MADE PLAY

A Dramabook

HILL AND WANG

NEW YORK

COPYRIGHT © 1967 BY JOHN RUSSELL TAYLOR

ALL RIGHTS RESERVED

PUBLISHED IN THE UNITED STATES OF AMERICA

BY HILL AND WANG, INC.

STANDARD BOOK NUMBER (CLOTHBOUND EDITION): 8090-8230-6

STANDARD BOOK NUMBER (PAPERBACK EDITION): 8090-0546-8

LIBRARY OF CONGRESS CATALOG CARD NUMBER: 67-25684

FIRST AMERICAN EDITION OCTOBER 1967

FIRST DRAMABOOK EDITION AUGUST 1969

MANUFACTURED IN THE UNITED STATES OF AMERICA

2 3 4 5 6 7 8 9 0

Contents

Introduction

Not long ago I was talking with a group of young British dramatists about the theatre and play-writing in general. The term 'well-made play' came up, as it will, in a derogatory sense, and suddenly one of them said 'Come to think of it, why shouldn't a play be well-made? What's wrong with that?' What indeed. And yet the phrase, which seems obviously designed as a compliment, is almost invariably used in modern criticism as an insult. There must be a reason for this strange transformation, and the main purpose of this book is to look again at the whole history of how and why the term was devalued in this way, and to consider how far, in allowing it to be devalued, we have lost sight of certain vital elements in the theatre which deserve to be reconsidered.

I have confined myself largely to the British theatre because that is where, for most of us, the problem presents itself in its most acute form. Also, because the British theatre has remained surprisingly self-contained, and foreign influences, when they have counted for anything, have been slow in making themselves felt. Of course the shadows of Scribe and Sardou flit across these pages and so, later, does that of Ibsen. But centrally this is the story of how British drama developed, largely according to its own lights, from Tom Robertson to Terence Rattigan, by way of Henry Arthur Jones and Pinero, Wilde, Maugham, Lonsdale, Galsworthy and Noël Coward. Also, by implication, of how those in their various ways on the other side – Shaw, Yeats, Perfect Wagnerites, Quintessential Ibsenites, Gordon Craig – shaped, directed and finally helped to destroy this particular tradition, with results both good and bad for British drama today.

It is an odd story, with complexities and cross-currents we are only just beginning to see. But to tell it properly, it is necessary to start at the beginning.

Some French Preceptors

The beginning, of course, is to consider what we mean by the well-made play, and what at other times other people have meant by it. To find this out we have to look for a theory of the well-made play, and to find a theory we have to look, as usual, not to Britain but to the Continent. British writers always tend to do first, and to theorize, if at all, afterwards; consequently we find them writing well-made plays long before they had decided, or had it decided for them, that that is what they were doing. No, for a coherent theory of what the well-made play was and ought to be, we must turn instead to France, and to the inventor of the form, Eugène Scribe.

Nothing comes from nothing, and certainly all sorts of precursors can be found for Scribe and his form of play. But for our purpose it is sufficient to say that what had been done occasionally, patchily and empirically by others Scribe did regularly, consistently and in full consciousness of what he was doing. He was born in 1791, and his first play appeared in 1815. By this time he had already been in the theatre for some years, and had learnt more about the sheer *technique* of catching and holding an audience than many much greater dramatists learn in their whole working lives. His prime originality lay in his realization that the most reliable formula for holding an audience's attention was a well-told story. Note the well-*told*; Scribe was living in the first heyday of Romanticism, and his theory of drama was not, could not be, a classical one of balance and proportion in the construction of an intrigue. To appreciate fully what Scribe meant by a *pièce bien faite* one must always bear this in mind; that what he set out to do was not to tame and discipline Romantic extravagance, but to devise a mould into which any sort of material, however extravagant and seemingly uncontrollable, could be poured.

He saw that all drama, in performance, is an experience in time, and that therefore the first essential is to keep one's audience attentive from one minute to the next. Romantic drama tended to neglect this requirement, or at least do little deliberately to satisfy it. Which was all very well if, say, the central character was so absorbing that an audience was willing to go along with anything that he or she did, or if the big scenes of spectacle and sensation were so spectacular and so sensational that the audience would just sit there and wait for the next to cap the last. But these were unduly chancy considerations, depending upon the author's qualities of imagination or at least of sheer invention. For a poet or novelist who might dabble in the theatre when he felt in the mood – or 'inspired' – to do so, they could well be enough. But a full-time professional playwright needed something more certain to go by.

This something was what Scribe provided. His plays inculcated, not the overall construction of a drama such as Racine would have understood it, but at least the spacing and preparation of effects so that an audience should be kept expectant from beginning to end. That, and that only, is what Scribe meant by a well-made play, and it is, if not perhaps the most one might hope for from a playwright, at least a very proper and by no means despicable minimum. Naturally, the exact way that Scribe realized his aim of the *pièce bien faite* varies somewhat from play to play, but his works are essentially built very much to formula – as one would expect, considering that between 1815 and his death in 1861 he wrote, alone or in collaboration, some 500 plays.

To understand that formula, and to see exactly how other writers made use of it, adapted it, modified it to suit their own ends, and especially gave it a deeper and more serious interpretation than ever occurred to Scribe, the best way, no doubt, is to examine in detail one of the plays in which Scribe used it to the best effect.

Let us take one of Scribe's largest and most lasting successes, *Adrienne Lecouvreur*, which he wrote with Ernest Legouvé in

1849. The drama is set in Paris in 1730. The central characters of the plot are Adrienne herself, a rising young actress at the Comédie-Française, her lover Maurice, Comte de Saxe, and Maurice's former mistress the Princesse de Bouillon. In the opening scenes, between the Princesse and an attendant Abbé and then between the Princesse and Maurice, we learn that the Princesse's husband is having an affair with the actress of the moment, la Duclos, that the Princesse is having an affair with Maurice, and that she is jealous when he arrives to see him wearing a small bouquet given to him (in for the moment thoroughly innocent circumstances) by la Duclos's new rival Adrienne Lecouvreur. Pretending to think the flowers are for her, she dismisses Maurice and commissions the ever-ready Abbé to find out who Maurice's new love may be; but he innocently hands on the job to the Princesse's husband.

All that in the first act. The audience, by now eager to see how this entanglement may unravel itself, have to wait a little in the second act while they watch the relationship between Adrienne and Maurice flower during a scene in which she undertakes to improve his French by reciting to him La Fontaine's fable 'Les Deux Pigeons'. After this the Prince de Bouillon arrives at the theatre, and through a misunderstanding decides that Maurice is in fact conducting an intrigue with *his* mistress, la Duclos, who has acted of late as a messenger between Maurice and the Princesse. The Prince therefore arranges for a reception at la Duclos's house, to which all the Comédie Française are invited and at which Maurice will be present (the Prince's aim being to catch Maurice and la Duclos together; not realizing that the rendezvous is in fact between Maurice and his wife); Adrienne agrees to come.

The third act begins with the meeting between Maurice and the Princesse, who has come to tell him some disturbing news of a debt he must pay if his political ambitions are not to be adversely affected. When the Prince, the Abbé and Adrienne arrive, as arranged, the Princesse takes refuge in a neighbouring room. Adrienne, introduced to Maurice (whose real identity she has not known before) takes his good faith on trust and agrees to aid him by giving the unknown lady visitor a key with which she can make her escape through the garden. The two women do not come face to face, as it is dark; but the Princesse hears and remembers Adrienne's voice, while she drops a bracelet in her flight, which is given to Adrienne. The Abbé comfortingly assures the Prince that whoever the unknown woman was, she was not la Duclos; Adrienne, on hearing that Maurice has fled, apparently after the unknown woman, faints as the curtain falls.

At the beginning of Act Four, Maurice has been in prison for debt, largely owing to the jealous treachery of the Princesse. But when he is released, through the generous intervention of Adrienne, who has pawned her jewels to pay his debt, he presumes that his anonymous benefactor was the Princesse, and goes to thank her. At the Princesse's he meets Adrienne, who has been invited there to recite at a social gathering. Face to face at last, the two women recognize each other from the Princesse's bracelet, Adrienne's voice, and, once Maurice and the Prince are safely shunted out of the room, get down to the *scène à faire*, cutting into each other with bitter irony. Adrienne, infuriated by the attention the Princesse pays Maurice, hits back by choosing to recite one of Phèdre's tirades about the seemingly innocent face which crime can put on. For the moment she is triumphant in the Princesse's confusion, but already the Princesse is urgently plotting revenge.

This comes in full measure in Act Five. The Princesse, who still has the bouquet Adrienne first sent to Maurice, sends it back to Adrienne impregnated with poison. Adrienne is in despair, assuming that it comes from Maurice and signifies that he has abandoned her, and breathes deeply of the poison. Maurice, having found out from the Princesse that she was largely responsible for his imprisonment, comes to justify his subsequent behaviour to Adrienne. Here he discovers from Adrienne's faithful friend Michonnet that it was Adrienne who paid for his release, and Adrienne and he fall into each other's arms. But too late; the poison is already taking effect, and after a lengthy scene of anguished avowals Adrienne expires in her lover's arms.

Now that, even on very cursory examination, does not look

much like what we would normally think of as a well-made play. The events crowd in one after another, with no time for the spectator to catch his breath, promising no more than a new thrill in the immediately following scene. Admittedly one or two things carry over to bind the play together, particularly that rather improbable bouquet that causes all the trouble. But of more sophisticated construction there is none, it is a case of 'Nothing but bonfires' as one sensation follows another. No very marked attempt to disguise the component parts, either: exposition is presented shamelessly as such, and characters such as the Abbé and Michonnet are introduced without the slightest qualms entirely in order to tell us things. Even the Prince de Bouillon and his shadowy mistress la Duclos are there mainly to help press the play forward from one big scene to another by complicating matters beyond all reason.

On the other hand, the play does fulfil triumphantly the prime requirement of Scribe's theatre: its story, however preposterous, is extremely well told, so that there is not one moment in the whole evening when the audience is not in a state of eager expectation, waiting for something to happen, for some secret to be uncovered, some identity revealed, some inevitable confrontation actually to occur. Scribe's art, above all, is the art of making connections, and beyond that for all he is concerned construction can go hang. Construction, the nice balancing of part by part, is for literature; but theatre is something different, a matter of immediate experience. Nor does what may or may not, on careful, reasonable consideration, appear probable or even possible matter to Scribe in the slightest: he is interested only in what an audience will or will not accept in the heat of the moment.

We are here, then, still a far cry from what Pinero, say, would have regarded as the well-made play. For essential to the well-made play of the 1890s, the sort of play Archer analyses in his book *Play-Making*, are two elements Scribe was not really interested in at all: clear, neat, balanced overall construction, and the appearance at least of verisimilitude. If Scribe was a crucial influence in putting serious British dramatic writing back into the theatre after too long spent in Elizabethan closets, the particular way that this new theatricalism found expression was specifically English. It was guided above all by the bourgeois realism of Tom Robertson, who took Scribe's unashamedly non-literary approach to dramatic story-telling and applied it to commonplace elements of contemporary middle-class life in a fashion which prompted Archer to call him, not unfairly, 'a Pre-Raphaelite of the theatre'.

But French drama did not stop short with Scribe, and neither did French influence in England. After Scribe came Victorien Sardou (1831–1908), the prime *bête noire* of those who favoured Ibsen and the new drama of ideas. Sardou began as Scribe's disciple, scoring his first great success with *Les Pattes de Mouche* (1860), and thereafter churned out a succession of plays almost as long as his master's. But Sardou had a more orderly mind than Scribe, and went on to define the older dramatist's notions of formula theatre into something far neater and more precise – and easier to copy. All his plays, whether comic or dramatic, lush costume dramas or allegedly realistic treatments of current problems, fall much into the same mould: a short, sharp exposition, in which we are introduced to the dramatis personae and learn all we need to know of their previous history, followed by a section devoted to misunderstandings, secrets which cannot be revealed, lost papers, intercepted messages and the like, leading up to one or more *scènes à faire*: the confrontation which every theatregoer has been led to expect as the logical climax of the story, towards which the whole creation moves. Ideally this should seem inevitable, but, Sardou reasons, if a few licenses have to be taken with the requirements of strict probability, who is going to complain provided the big scene at the end justifies the means by which it is reached? And after the *scène à faire*, the *dénouement*, the unravelling of the plot – to be accomplished as quickly as possible, and with the maximum of sensational effect in the way of last-minute revelation, spectacular conversion or something of the sort.

Most of Sardou's most famous pieces, which still survive as names if nothing else, were historical dramas, several written for Bernhardt – *Fédora* (1882), *Théodora Impératrice de Byzance* (1884), *La Tosca* (1887) remembered through Puccini's opera,

Cléopâtre (1890), *Gismonda* (1894) and *Madame Sans-Gêne* (1893), a collaboration with Émile Moreau which still bears occasional revival. This last contains more comedy than heavy drama, and there are in fact a number of comedies among Sardou's works, but his reputation and influence, then and since, were based almost entirely on his 'consummate craftsmanship' (Sydney Grundy's phrase) in the design of popular drama.

The other side of the coin was presented by Eugène Labiche (1815–1888), Sardou's nearest counterpart among specialists in comedy. Labiche, like Scribe and Sardou, was vastly prolific, alone or in collaboration, and specialized above all in farces which led their characters, once embarked on some complicated intrigue, into one adventure after another, each prefaced by some tantalizing setting-up in the previous scene, and each capping what has come before with bigger laughs instead of, as in Scribe, bigger thrills. The perfect example is Labiche's most famous farce, *Un Chapeau de paille d'Italie* (1851), in which a young man finds himself in difficulties when his horse happens to eat the hat of a lady who ought not to be anywhere near at the time and he is led on a dizzying chase trying to find her one just like it before her husband finds out.

As Scribe stands to Sardou, so does Labiche to Feydeau. Georges Feydeau (1862–1921) took the discursive, expansive farce of Labiche and shaped it into clockwork regularity. In his characteristic plays pattern is all; verbal wit and characterization are entirely subjugated to it. Nothing could be neater or more beautifully, economically shaped than *Occupe-toi d'Amélie* (1908) *Un fil a la patte* (1894) or *La Pouce à l'Oreille* (1907): mechanical their obsessively symmetrical plots undoubtedly are, and yet the machinery is so meticulously finished, and works with such hypnotic precision, that the craft becomes art, a triumph of pure style, a self-defining mechanism which carries pure theatre to the edge of Theatre of the Absurd, and sometimes over.

Scribe, Sardou and to a lesser extent Labiche were constantly translated or adapted into English, imitated by the English playwrights of the 1870s and 1880s, and held up by conservatives to proponents of the New Drama as models of craftsmanship.

Feydeau came later, and was too highly personal, and in every sense, conventional and otherwise, too 'French' a writer for the British to learn much from him. The British well-made play, as it turned out, developed in a very different direction from the French *pièce bien faite* – something much nearer, if one must have a French comparison, to Dumas fils and his famous emotional drama *La Dame aux Camélias*, for long unproduceable in England. But even that is ultimately remote in its effect from the drama of Robertson, of Henry Arthur Jones, and of Arthur Wing Pinero. The French model remained in front of them, but their Englishness transformed what they learned from it into something very different. And the first dramatist to do this was T. W. Robertson.

Tom Robertson and the 1870s

It has long been normal to date the realistic reform in the English theatre from the advent of T. W. (Tom) Robertson. And while this is on nearly all counts an over-simplification, it remains all the same a reasonable one to start with, mainly because, whether on strict and careful study of Robertson's predecessors and how he differed from them we conclude that his 'revolution' was as radical as people thought, the important thing is that at the time many influential in the theatre thought so and acted accordingly.

What Robertson was (and is) famed for above all is having introduced on to the mid-Victorian stage a realistic picture of everyday middle-class life. Well, of course the term is relative. To us, now, Robertson's plots seem often hardly less improbable and melodramatic than those of the unashamed melodramas he was reacting against, while his plays abound in such conventions as soliloquy, aside and simultaneous conversations on stage by characters who are supposed not to be aware of each other's presence. Nor was Robertson the first dramatist of his age to deal with current social problems in what was meant to be a realistic way – even Lord Lytton, author of the most phenomenally successful romantic melodrama of the period, *The Lady of Lyons* (1838), also dabbled, according to his lights, with everyday realism in plays like *Money* (1840), the very title of which has a Robertson-like ring.

But undoubtedly Robertson went further in this direction, wrote better while doing so, and hit exactly the right moment for doing so – hence his historical importance, even if as a dramatist he remains very much in the minor league. He was born in 1829, his family background including a number of actors, writers, painters and professional artists of various sorts.

He himself went on the stage in early childhood, and continued to act with modest success for some years. He also had the itch to write, however, and seemed all set for early success when a play of his, *A Night's Adventure*, was accepted for production by a major London company in 1851.

But though this piece of period flummery about Jacobites, Hanoverians and a romantic highwayman in disguise was in no way challenging and was by all accounts in general rather better than the run of such plays at the time, it had no success at all, and its unfortunate author was reduced to churning out innumerable adaptations, mainly 'from the French'. Among those he wrote in the mid-1850s were, significantly perhaps, *The Ladies' Battle* from *La bataille des dames*, by Scribe and Legouvé, and *A Glass of Water*, from Scribe's *Un Verre d'eau*. Thus the great innovator-to-be was thoroughly familiar with Scribe's work and methods some years before his own major original successes were written, and no doubt learnt from them quite a lot about Scribe's concept of the *pièce bien faite*, which was as we have seen above all the art of telling a story to maximum effect in specifically theatrical terms.

Robertson's first success with a play of his own did not come until 1864, by which time he had completely given up acting for writing and spent some time as a drama critic, of the *Illustrated Times*. And even the first play to make any sort of a name for him, *David Garrick*, was in fact an adaptation, admittedly free, from a French play, de Melesville's *Sullivan*, which in its turn was only one of many variations on the old notion of a stage star deliberately disenchanting an infatuated young admirer by cutting a very unflattering figure off-stage. The main thing which distinguishes the play from any number of others cast in a similar mould is the love-scene in the last act, which though inevitably sentimental has a lightness and charm which convinced audiences at the time that it was very true to life – or at any rate a good deal truer than most of what they were currently offered on the stage.

Girded with this success Robertson went on almost at once to offer an original play of his own: *Society*, written in 1864 and produced in November 1865. This had a resounding success, and marked Robertson's definitive arrival as the dramatist of the day, especially when confirmed by the success of *Ours* in 1866 and *Caste*, his most famous play, in 1867. These slight, graceful, rather silly plays do not look much like the start of revolution, and it does not seem to have been a vital part of Robertson's purpose to call anyone in the theatre to arms. Indeed here even Pinero's funny, nostalgic and not essentially innaccurate picture of Robertson in *Trelawny of the Wells* errs somewhat; Robertson wrote what his nature made him write, not in response to any doctrinaire programme.

Certainly *Society*, for all its air of novelty in 1865, does not now seem very revolutionary unless we think ourselves back carefully into the historical context. The story itself is full of devices straight out of Scribe. The Chodd family, rich but far from aristocratic, decide to enter society – as a first step towards which John Chodd Jr. is to get elected to Parliament. With this in view his father hires a 'literary barrister' called Sidney Daryl to run a newspaper supporting the candidate, and this brings on to the scene Daryl's sweetheart Maud Hetherington, who immediately attracts Chodd Jr's attentions. Her aunt, Lady Ptarmigant, supports Chodd's suit, since he is rich and Daryl is poor; Maud does not oppose her because, owing to a conveniently contrived misunderstanding, she has taken it into her head that Daryl's ward is in fact his daughter. Daryl in his turn, hearing at a gathering in the Owls' Roost, a bohemian pub, that Maud is engaged to Chodd, is first reduced to quiet despair and then, in a rousing second-act curtain scene, accuses her of shameless double-dealing during a ball at Lady Ptarmigant's house and leaves her fainting. To fight back he enters the election in competition with Chodd and wins. At last all is revealed: the mysterious ward is really Lady Ptarmigant's grand-daughter, orphan child of a scapegrace son, nobly protected by Daryl. Moreover, he comes in for a last-minute legacy, and so all obstacle to his marriage with Maud is removed.

The machinery is quite obviously that of the *pièce bien faite*: the very slightly-based misunderstanding – Maud, hearing little Maud refer to herself as 'Mr. Daryl's little girl', automatically assumes the bachelor Daryl must be her father, and makes no further inquiries – the secret about parentage, the 'strong' curtain tableau, even the *deus ex machina* with a bequest of money out of the blue. But audiences and critics who believed they were seeing something new in the British theatre were not mistaken. First, and most importantly, there is Robertson's way with dialogue. In *Society* he has not yet perfectly mastered his style, but it is still plain enough what he is doing: in place of the prevalent rhetorical style – of Scribe as much as of the normal British drama at the time – he adopts a light, intimate style of short speeches, each one taking up the thread of what has gone before in an easy, natural-seeming way. The characters seem, in fact, to be listening to and answering each other rather than speaking to the audience or at least primarily for the audience's benefit.

This imposes a natural, unemphatic style of acting on the players, and, moreover, requires them to play as an ensemble rather than as so many individuals waiting to deliver their big speeches. The style is not quite consistently maintained: the opening exposition is a little clumsily managed, and big effects like Daryl's denunciation of Maud in the second act fall into melodrama. But enough is there to signal the arrival of a new voice in the theatre and indeed a whole new approach to the business of drama. Even conventions like the simultaneous presentation of two actions independent of each other in the same scene are turned to account: the cross-cutting of Daryl's electoral address with a duologue between Maud and Chodd Jr. broadly but effectively breaks up any possibility of a big rhetorical effect, and points the way to Robertson's far subtler use of the same device in later plays. And if Robertson shows in it little originality as a social thinker, at least he does manage to come up with rough but believable exchanges like this, between rich and poor suitors:

CHODD JR: . . . Capital commands the world. The capitalist commands capital, therefore the capitalist commands the world.

SIDNEY: But you don't quite command the world, do you?

CHODD JR: Practically, I do. I wish for the highest honours –

I bring out my cheque-book. I want to go into the House of Commons – cheque book. I want the best legal opinion in the House of Lords – cheque book. The best house – cheque book. The best turn-out – cheque book. The best friends, the best wife, the best-trained children – cheque book, cheque book and cheque book.

The great success of *Society* went far to type Robertson as writer of the sort of play by which he is now (if at all) remembered: the romantic comedy-drama of middle-class life, with the upper and lower orders impinging from time to time. As to how far it went in ruthless realism, *The Daily Telegraph* reviewing the first production of *Society* reached a conclusion which still seems fair and valid:

> Those who demand a subtle analysis of human motives, and require an elaborate dissection of the various component parts of the social body, must seek opportunities for acquiring knowledge elsewhere; but people who care about seeing a clever, sketchy picture of modern men and manners, dashed off in a spirited style, and giving, perhaps, a new view of some gradations in the social scale, may include themselves among the throng who nightly gather round the portals of the cheerful little theatre in Tottenham Street, and make sure of not coming away disappointed.

That is a reasonable judgement: the plots of Robertson's plays may be full of contrivance, and nothing in them goes very deep, but they are constantly illuminated by little insights, strokes of irony which give an edge to the sentiment and do after all remind us of a reality beyond the walls of the theatre. In *Society* the key scene as far as the play's success was concerned was the least conventional: that at the Owls' Roost, which surprised audiences both by the detailed realism of its setting and by the way that its final dramatic effect was underplayed. Here is the opening direction:

> Parlour at the 'Owls' Roost' public house. Cushioned seats all round the apartment; gas lighted on each side over tables; splint boxes, pipes, newspapers, etc., on table, writing

materials on table (near door); gong bell on another table; door of entrance near centre; clock above door (hands set to half past nine); hat pegs and coats on walls.

And the action within this setting is equally realistic – or so at any rate the journalists who were feared likely to take offence at it found – and the conclusion is a sharp break with melodramatic tradition. Daryl, one of the revellers, gathers from something which is said that Maud is engaged to his rival, Chodd. Admittedly later, at the ball, he is to have his moment of melodrama over this, but for the moment nothing could be quieter and more restrained. He just starts slightly at the news, and when asked by a friend what is wrong he says 'Nothing'. Then, as the attention of the other club-members switches elsewhere, with a song about how fickle women are, he sits silently at a table and then sinks his head on his hands in a despairing gesture as the curtain falls.

This way of building drama by underplaying it, so novel in the theatre of the 1860s, scored such a success that Robertson knew he was on the right track and exploited it further in *Ours*, the first play he wrote specifically for the Bancroft company. This is a more expertly written play, but suffers from much more improbability in the overall plot. It takes place during the Crimean War, which provides a lightly sketched-in background for three romantic stories: those of Blanche Haye, a young woman being pressed by her guardian Lady Shendryn to marry a rich Russian prince but in love with a poor and diffident Scot; Blanche's friend Mary Netley, who has a sparring love-relationship with the initially effete but eventually heroic Hugh Chalcot; and Lady Shendryn, an unreasonably jealous woman who constantly suspects her husband of infidelity. The plots are set up in England and resolved in the Crimea, when the ladies turn up in conditions of unlikely comfort and convenience to care for their menfolk and see them through unscathed. It may seem curious to us that the play's original audiences, many in which had personal reason to see the Crimea in a grimmer light, should have accepted this all so readily (the play was more profitable than any Robertson except *Caste*). But no doubt the reason for this was largely the great skill with which Robertson disposed the elements of his comedy, and particularly the ease with which he varied its pace, using to great effect the technique of the election scene in *Society* to set the timid young lovers Blanche and Angus against the bickering of Blanche's guardians in the first act and against the easy bonhomie of Chalcot with the rest in the third.

In *Caste*, the most famous of all Robertson's plays, the method was developed still further. For one thing, there is rather less in the way of plot, so that the characters of the principals can expand at will. Esther Eccles, a young actress, has married George d'Alroy, a handsome young aristocrat who promptly goes off to war and gets himself killed. Most of the play is occupied with the battle of Esther to keep her child and to keep her from d'Alroy's insufferably snobbish mother, the Marquise de St. Maure. In this she is sorely tried by her reprobate father, a boozy old monster who won't work and does nothing but make trouble for everybody – the character is one of Robertson's liveliest. Meanwhile her sister Polly is engaged in a contrasting romance with Sam Gerridge, a respectable workman who believes that everyone ought to keep to his place. In the end George comes back, unharmed, Esther and her child are welcomed into the family by the Marquise, and everything ends in a welter of charmingly sentimental contrivance. But even here, right at the end of the piece, the happy girl and his sister soliloquize thus:

ESTER (*aside*): And she will live in a back room behind a shop. Well – I hope she will be happy.
POLLY (*aside*): And she will live in a fine house, and have a carriage, and be a lady. Well – I hope she will be happy.

The whole play, with its adroit mixing of comedy and sentiment, its light, easy movement and its air of naturalness even when most obviously contrived, has a sort of Mendelssohnian grace and charm which keeps it obstinately alive and fresh when by any reasonable judgment it should be hopelessly faded by now. It is perhaps the high point of Robertson's career – certainly most people then and since have agreed in finding it that. Apparently Robertson thought so too; in any case, having found his style and company, and having confirmed his hold on his audience, he went on writing in much the same vein. Not exclusively, though. So far was he from being doctrinaire about his realistic revolution that in various plays after *Ours*, he showed every willingness to try his hand at old-style melodrama: in *Shadow Tree Shaft* (1867), for instance, in *For Love, or, The Two Heroes* (1867), which was suggested in part by the wreck of the Birkenhead, and in *The Nightingale* (1870), a demented fantasy involving scheming orientals, sopranos inclined to insanity while under stress and a full-scale flood for the sake of stage spectacle – all irresistibly pilloried by W. S. Gilbert in the pages of *Fun*. But try as he might, this sort of play was just not in his line: his graceful love-scenes, subtleties of characterization and occasional shafts of satirical wit – everything in fact which went to make up what one of his biographers called, not unfairly, his 'delicate and scholarly style' – went for nothing and less than nothing, proving positively destructive to the sturdier pleasures which might be expected from melodrama.

His realistic comedy-dramas, however, continued to show a ripening and maturing of the style he had made his own. His next piece for the Bancrofts, *Play* (1868), wandered a little away from it, setting its slightly melodramatic plot in a German gambling resort and varying the simple central love-story with touches of spectacle and interludes of comedy broad to the verge of farce. But *School* (1869) retrieved the situation: it is the slightest, most delicate and tender of all Robertson's plays, a spring-song by Mendelssohn with hardly any plot to speak of and its realism dissolved into a haze of romantic enchantment. It is based remotely on a German play, Roderick Benedix's *Aschenbrödel*, a rather heavy rehandling of the Cinderella story. In Robertson's hands it becomes a romantic comedy about Bella and Naomi, two teachers in a girls' school, and the romantic confusions they produce in the hearts of the neighbouring young gentry. Lord Beaufoy is encouraged by his uncle Percy Farintosh to cultivate their company in the hope that he will fall for Naomi, who happens to be an heiress. But of course instead romance blossoms between him and Bella. The romance gets Bella sent away from the school, but Lord Beaufoy goes after her to London, marries her and brings her back – to the news that she has all along been Farintosh's long-lost granddaughter.

Nothing to it at all, in fact, except that Robertson, by now completely master of his craft, lets it run along almost entirely on atmosphere, on the unforced charm of the relations between the young people, and on the knowing touches of eccentric characterization among their elders. Nowhere else is his dialogue so simple and natural: he carefully took the advice of his eleven-year-old son on what sort of answers he would give a teacher if meaning to be pert, and had the astuteness to break up the looming melodrama of a scene in which Bella receives an unwelcome proposal from the odious tutor Krux by having her scream 'Oh, don't!' – and then add, more realistically ' – on such a nice day as this!'

By this time Robertson came to write his last play for the Bancrofts, *M.P.* (1870), he was already ill and exhausted from his busy life as a writer, which had included during the five years of his association with the company at least fourteen other plays, several of them adaptations from the French and none at all comparable with his six Bancroft plays. The last few scenes of *M.P.* had to be dictated, as he was too ill to write, and the rehearsals were conducted in his home as he could not come to the theatre. In the circumstances it might be expected that the play would show no advance, and it does not show any very noticeably, though one or two scenes bring Robertson's technique of cutting back and forth from one conversation to another to a new degree of complexity. On the other hand *M.P.* shows no falling off: the rather involved plot is handled with great skill and the characterization, if like all Robertson's characterization based on the modification in detail of clearly recognizable stereotypes, is an accomplished as ever in ringing the necessary changes.

The story is again one of social degree and romantic impulses which cut across. The Dunscombe estates are passing to a rich parvenu, Isaac Skoome, and to make matters worse Dunscombe

Dunscombe's son Chudleigh falls in love with Skoome's ward Ruth instead of his cousin Cecilia, the choice of his father. Meanwhile Cecilia falls in love with Talbot Piers, Skoome's opponent in a parliamentary election, and pays from her own bank account a necessary bribe which he is too high-principled to countenance. Finding that £2,000 of her money has gone Piers at once assumes that Dunscombe has taken it to aid Skoome; Cecilia finds this unforgivable and they quarrel. Meanwhile Chudleigh runs away with Ruth, who was destined to be Skoome's bride; Skoome loses the election to Piers, and Piers and Cecilia are reunited.

So ended, prematurely, Robertson's career as a dramatist. As will be seen, his revolution, if such it may be called, was less a full-scale attack on the sort of theatre then in vogue than a significant refinement, a modification of detail. He had learnt technical adroitness from Scribe, and there is no doubt that in the art of telling a story in dramatic terms, keeping the audience *au fait* with what had gone before and panting to know what would happen next, he had few if any rivals in the contemporary English theatre. But by temperament he was not fitted to the wilder flights of melodrama, and so instead he applied this talent to altogether quieter, more everyday material than his mentor usually chose, paying more attention to atmosphere and individual characterization. The result of these two small modifications – the systematic application of Scribe-like technique and the concentration on contemporary middle-class British life for subject-matter – taken together was a new and influential genre: the British realistic well-made play. Perhaps, as has been suggested, Robertson himself imagined that his plays were a brusque English answer to the *pièce bien faite* as established by Sardou, but if so this would be yet another example of how little authors tend to know about the precise nature and sources of their art.

But the influence Robertson was to have in the next couple of decades came only partly from his writing *per se*. For Robertson was perhaps even more influential as a 'stage manager' – director, as we would now say – than as a writer. Though at this time the director in the modern sense was unknown in Britain,

Robertson made a point – as long as his health allowed him, which was to within a year or so of his death in 1871 – of supervising the production of his own plays in very close detail. To begin with the physical setting of the production did not always match the realistic intentions of the text. The *Pall Mall Gazette*, reviewing *Society* in 1865, remarked that

> In a comedy which aims at realism, and the essential character of which demands *vraisemblance*, the furniture and accessories are of great importance. For these the author is not altogether accountable. Few dramatists are allowed to be stage-managers, and one does not expect to find in Tottenham Court Road the elegance which Madame Vestris exhibited at the Lyceum; but we may reasonably expect to see a fashionable drawing-room in the 'noble mansion' of Lord Ptarmigant furnished with more than one chair and with a carpet of visible proportions, especially as there are some allusions to the wealth of the British nobleman.

How far this particular deficiency was the result of carelessness and how far simple lack of funds does not seem to be recorded. But what is certain is that Robertson determined that there should be no ground for criticism of this sort again. In *Ours*, the following year, a particular impression seems to have been created by the effect of snow driving into a hut in the Crimea (the background was nothing if not topical) every time the door was opened, but this sort of obtrusive special effect was no great novelty in the theatre. On the other hand *Caste*, the year after, had such refinements on current theatrical practice as sets with ceilings, doors with locks and windows with glass. The advantages, if any, of this can be, and have been, endlessly debated, but undoubtedly at the time such details were considered important, a great stride towards greater stage realism. And this, not because individually they were entirely without precedent, but because they were introduced less as obtrusive production-gimmicks than as part of the whole production's fabric of realism.

Allied with these visual refinements was Robertson's close concern for the style in which his pieces were played. The company for which most of his best plays were written, that run by the Bancrofts, was at this time young, forward-looking, admiring of their author and unusually amenable when it came to instruction. So he found himself in a position to instruct, and his methods at rehearsal have been constantly cited as exemplary by other writers and actors who worked with him. In the 1890s W. S. Gilbert wrote that he regarded 'stage-management as now understood, as having been absolutely "invented" by Robertson', and John Hare, a distinguished alumnus of the Bancroft company who specialized in the portrayal of old men, said that 'As nature was the basis of his own work, so he sought to make actors understand it should be theirs. He thus founded a school of natural acting which completely revolutionized the then existing methods, and by so doing did incalculable good to ths stage.'

Thus it was that Robertson's impact on the theatre was as concentrated as it was: the modifications he introduced might be small enough taken one by one, but they all hung together and represented a novel way of looking at the theatre. His own style of writing worked well only in his own kind of play, and his own kind of play worked well only with his own kind of player. But when everything was favourable, as it was especially in his happy association with the Bancrofts, it all worked so spectacularly well that it imposed itself as a model for intelligent English drama for some time to come, and even when Robertson came to seem as old-fashioned to Pinero as Lytton had seemed to him and as Pinero seemed to Shaw, his example was still revered as the only begetter of the realistic English drama which flourished in his wake.

Not that, as far as the writing side of drama was concerned, this flourished very spectacularly for nearly twenty years after Robertson's death. His way of writing was too personal and idiosyncratic to find many followers, and the Bancrofts, while always on the look-out for a new Robertson, found themselves compelled to keep reviving Robertson's plays as the centre-pieces of their modern repertory. But something at least did rub off on the dramatists of the 1870s and 1880s: Robertson's plays, and the way the Bancrofts played them, had done much to abolish for ever the rigid categorization of roles in British drama, with the hero, heroine, villain, soubrette, low comedian, old father, etc. each the province of a particular player in a stock company, and each played in much the same rigidly stereotyped way from play to play. Robertson, whatever his drawbacks as a depictor of character, at least believed that every character in a play should be written as an individual, and played as such, without any automatic reference to 'the usually recognized lines of business'. This the Bancroft company put triumphantly into effect, and from 1870 on the concept of every role a character role became standard, at least in the respectable, 'serious' theatre.

The trouble was, there was so little of it in the works of the newer dramatists. One of two of the old dogs showed a passing willingness to learn new tricks: the perennial Tom Taylor (1817–1880), author of such long-lasting and still enjoyable melodramas as *Still Waters Run Deep* (1855) and *The Ticket-of-Leave Man* (1863), took a few tentative steps in the direction of Robertsonian social drama in such later plays as *New Men and Old Acres* (1869), which deals with the displacement of some poor aristocrats from their ancestral home by a newly rich self-made man. But even this was only a temporary aberration on Taylor's part: the bulk of his output during the 1870s was made up of fustian historical dramas as remote as possible from Robertson's theory and practice.

James Albery (1838–1889) at least looked for a while something like a serious disciple of Robertson. But his best play, *Two Roses* (1870), with its Robertsonian plot about a dispute over a title – the first pretentious claimant finds himself passed over in favour of the despised blind suitor of one of his daughters – and its freshness and lightness in the characterization of the rogue Digby Grant and his two daughters, turned out to be merely the prelude to a stage career of more superficial success with such plays as *Pink Dominos* (1877), long a byword for farcical foolishness.

The most interesting dramatist of the period immediately after Robertson's death, W. S. Gilbert (1836–1911), is really outside our field of consideration, for though in some of his early comedies he shows influence from Scribe and also possibly from Labiche, his most characteristic works are the fairy-fantasies which pave the way for the Gilbert-and-Sullivan operettas starting with *Trial by Jury* in 1875. The Savoy opera, though obviously more vital than any other product of the English theatre between Sheridan and Wilde, is of course *sui generis*, and its links with the well-made play tradition are only of the most tenuous.

Less interesting but more relevant are the two other leading dramatists of the period immediately after Robertson's death, his old friend H. J. Byron (1834–1884), and Sydney Grundy (1848–1914). Byron was charming and fertile, and shone particularly in burlesque. But apparently he grew tired of being noted entirely as a droll, and in 1868 took up the challenge to produce something more serious with *Cyril's Success*, which he proudly presented in his introduction to the printed text as 'effective in performance, and not altogether unworthy perusal ... original, and a comedy – and, even in these vicious dramatic days – in five acts!' As Pinero later remarked, it is difficult to see any particular advantage in five acts, except that the play 'has so many faults that it would not be possible for a smaller number of acts to contain them.' This is entirely fair: though the subject-matter, the marital difficulties of a successful playwright, has faint suggestions of Robertson, the characterization is straight from stock (the cast-list even assigns each character his traditional label: walking gentleman, character comedy, utility, juvenile comedy, chambermaid) and the plot is forwarded by coincidences and misunderstandings so preposterous that all suggestion of verisimilitude is soon entirely dismissed. Wisely, perhaps, Byron never ventured so boldly into 'serious' drama again, and his later farces, such as *Our Boys* (1875), while more engaging because less pretentious, have nothing noticeably to do with Robertson, the well-made play or anything else which might distinguish the English theatre of the 1870s from that of twenty or thirty years earlier.

Of Grundy as an original dramatist it is difficult to speak. What there is to be said for him, and the sort of drama he represents, has been said with much spirit by Grundy himself in his astonishing piece of rearguard action, *The Play of the Future: by a Playwright of the Past*, a booklet defending in the most uncompromising terms all the most retrograde elements of Victorian drama, published as late as 1914. The trouble is that Grundy was an adaptor par excellence. He belongs to that phase of the British theatre when 'from the French', though no less prevalent a label on new plays than before the advent of Robertson, had come to mean something far freer than mere translation. Grundy's sizeable output comprehends everything from the straight translation to the complete original, with infinite gradations of dependence in between. Among the French dramatists he laid under contribution were, inevitably, the old master Scribe and the new masters of the *pièce bien faite*, Sardou and Labiche. One of his major successes was *In Honour Bound* (1884), a sentimental drama skirting a tragedy adapted fairly closely from Scribe's immensely popular *Une Chaîne* (1891); and perhaps his most lastingly enjoyable work, *A Pair of Spectacles* (1890), was based, though here very loosely, on *Les Petits Oiseaux*, by Labiche and Delacour. This makes some crude but effective play with a piece of very elementary symbolism: when an impossibly trusting, benevolent old man breaks his old gold-rimmed spectacles and has to borrow the steel-rimmed spectacles of his misanthropic brother, he at once sees the world in the darkest possible terms, and is restored to good nature only when he regains his own glasses.

In his original plays, such as *A Fool's Paradise* (1892) and *Sowing the Wind* (1893), Grundy writes crudely melodramatic domestic dramas full of strong action and easy sentimentality, and much the same is true of one of his biggest successes, *A Bunch of Violets* (1894), adapted from Octave Feuillet's *Montjoye*. They are all notable for their clean, confident craftsmanship, as learnt from Grundy's avowed models Scribe and Sardou, and their total lack of any concern for the realities of English life with which Robertson had tried to turn Scribe's mechanical effects of story-telling technique to his own more intelligent ends. But anyway, by the beginning of the 1890s Grundy was already writing in a new context: the 'new drama', represented by Ibsen and advocated by a number of influential critics, was beginning to colour the ideas of a number of thinking play-goers, and Grundy regarded himself quite consciously as an upholder of old ideals of pure, fairly uncontroversial entertainment against the noxious tide of 'ideas' in the theatre. But before we go on to see exactly how the British theatre stood twenty years after Robertson's death we must look back a little to catch up on the beginnings of the most important of the new men, Henry Arthur Jones and Arthur Wing Pinero.

Henry Arthur Jones

In November 1882 a melodrama called *The Silver King* created something of a sensation in the London theatre; a new dramatist, Henry Arthur Jones, had arrived. The play, as a matter of fact, was not his own unaided work; it was credited as a joint production of himself and one H. A. Herman. But informed opinion then attributed to Jones the lion's share of the text, and a considerable amount of rather undignified bickering subsequently, involving Jones, Herman and the leading actor in the production, Wilson Barrett, tended finally to show that this was indeed the case. Anyway, it is a matter of no great moment. The play is, according to its lights, well constructed and written with some gift for crisp and economical dialogue. But it is not and does not pretend to be more than a good commercial melodrama, handling its subject – the plight of a man who wrongly believes himself to be a murderer – with a sure but quite superficial mastery of theatrical effect. It is a *pièce bien faite* as Scribe would have understood it, but not even remotely an English well-made play.

However, it still has some importance, in that it made Henry Arthur Jones a name to be reckoned with in the London theatre of the 1880s. It was vastly successful, and on its success was founded a prosperous career of some twenty years in the theatre before public taste veered away from the sort of play Jones stood for in the early 1900s. At the time of *The Silver King*'s first production he was 31; he had worked as a commercial traveller, and had already been writing plays on and off since a first, unproduced effort in 1869. A number of his one-act plays had in fact had some success with the critics and the public; no less august a literary figure than Matthew Arnold had expressed guarded admiration for a couple of privately-printed pieces Jones had sent him, and wrote an influential and in general very fair review of *The Silver King* in the *Pall Mall Gazette*:

The critics are right, therefore, in thinking that in this work they have something new and highly praiseworthy, though it is not exactly what they suppose. They have a sensational drama in which the diction and sentiments do not overstep the modesty of nature. In general, in drama of this kind, the diction and sentiments, like the incidents, are extravagant, impossible, transpontine; here they are not. This is a very great merit, a very great advantage. The imagination can lend itself to almost any incidents, however violent; but good taste will always revolt against transpontine diction and sentiments. Instead of giving to their audience transpontine diction and sentiments, Messrs. Jones and Herman give them literature. Faults there are in *The Silver King*; Denver's drunkenness is made too much of, his dream is superfluous, the peasantry are a little tiresome, Denver's triumphant exit from Black Brake Wharf puzzles us. But in general throughout the piece the diction and sentiments are natural, they have sobriety and propriety, they are literature. It is an excellent and hopeful sign to find playwrights capable of writing in this style, actors capable of rendering it, a public capable of enjoying it.

But even before this Jones had been seen by one or two percipient (or perhaps merely hopeful) people as a potential saviour of the English stage. Apropos of one of his early one-act plays, *A Clerical Error*, produced at the Court Theatre in 1879, Wilson Barrett wrote to Jones:

... The public are pining for a pure English comedy, with a pure story, in which the characters shall be English, with English ideas, and English feelings, honest, true men, and tender, loving women, and from which plague, pestilence, adultery, fornication, battle, murder, and sudden death shall be banished.

The author who can do in three acts what you have done in one in *A Clerical Error* will take as strong a stand now as Tom Robertson took years ago.

The characters must not preach virtue, let them act it, not spout self-denial but show it. The public taste is depraved no doubt, the more depraved the greater certainty of success for the man who will try to raise it. This seems paradoxical, but do not the most abandoned women, in their hearts, admire virtue most, the greatest cowards worship bravery, . . .

The call was clear, and corresponded very much with Jones's own ambitions. He was to revive the British theatre by combining the theatrical knowhow of Scribe with subject-matter which would mirror the realities of contemporary British life and therefore allow his works to rank as 'literature', as the sort of serious, respectable, and to a moderate extent thought-provoking, entertainment that a new generation of high-minded theatregoers was longing to see. Robertson had shown the way; it was Jones's duty to follow it.

This he was more than willing to do. Moreover, he was eager to propagandize his aims. In a letter to *The Daily News* in 1883 he defended the British audience in these terms:

The truth is that audiences want literature, they want poetry, but they do not want unactable, intractable imitations of Shakespeare's form, without his vitality. They want life, they want reality; they demand that the characters they see on the stage shall be, not the ghostly abstractions of the study, but living, breathing human beings, with good warm red blood in their veins.

Later that year, in an article for *The Nineteenth Century* entitled 'The Theatre and the Mob', he put it still more strongly:

. . . on inquiring why we have no national drama at all worthy of the name, at all to be compared with the advances we have made in the sister arts of poetry, music, and painting, we are met first of all by the fact that the drama is not merely an art, but it is also a competitor of music-halls, circuses, Madame Tussaud's, the Westminster Aquarium, and the Argyll Rooms. It is a hybrid, an unwieldy Siamese Twin, with two bodies, two heads, two minds, two dispositions, all of them, for the present, vitally connected. And one of these two bodies, dramatic art, is lean and pinched and starving, and has to drag about with it, wherever it goes, its fat, puffy, unwholesome, dropsical brother, popular amusement. And neither of them goes its own proper way in the world to its own proper end, but they twain waddle on in a path that leads nowhere in particular, the resultant of their several luggings and tuggings at each other.

But the demand for truth, for reality, for thought, for poetry, for all kinds of noble and inspiring examples, difficult as it may be to rear at the first, is yet perennial, constant, assured, and eternally fruitful. Every position of honour, every position really worth coveting in the dramatic world today, whether of manager, or actor, or author, has been gained, not by the base idea of catering for every passing appetite of the multitude, but by unflagging appeals to the nobler instincts of the few, by coaxing, by watching, by alluring, by guiding, by resolutely refusing to pander to the public. . . .

As might be expected from all this, he was himself preparing an attack on conventional standards in the theatre of his time, and in 1884 it appeared: *Saints and Sinners*. It is difficult now to realize the effect this superficial and melodramatic piece had on audiences and critics at the time. Its prime target is the hypocrisy lurking beneath the pious religious exteriors of certain members of the merchant classes: the 'ludicrous want of harmony, or apparently of even the most distant relation of any sort between a man's religious professions and his actions', as Jones puts in his preface to the published text. Jacob Fletcher, pastor of the local Bethel, comes into head-on collision with one of his deacons, Hoggard, a tanner, when he opposes Hoggard's attempts to have the widow of his former partner turned out of her home. He wins, but only at the expense of having Hoggard make public the scandal of his own daughter's seduction by heartless Captain Fanshawe. He is forced to resign, but has the satisfaction of being able to practise Christian charity on Hoggard by taking him in when, his double-dealings discovered, he becomes a fugitive from the law. Fanshawe gets his just deserts, Fletcher's daughter's true and faithful farmer suitor George Kingsmill comes back in the nick of time, and though Letty, having been once dishonoured, has to die conveniently before the final curtain, virtue is finally justified and vice suitably punished.

This all seems conventional enough; but in 1884 it did not strike people that way. We must remember that this was an era when Jones could have one of his one-act plays, *Welcome Little Stranger* (c. 1885), refused a licence by the Lord Chamberlain because it opened with a mysterious scene of comings and goings along a corridor which ended with a nurse coming in and announcing 'It is a fine boy'. The social criticism embodied in *Saints and Sinners* may have been elementary, but at the time it was regarded as something new in British drama, and daringly frank. Even the final dispatch of the unfortunate Letty, which seems to us the conventional moralizing conclusion (the wages of womanly sin, even if thoroughly repented afterwards, is bound to be death), was in the context of its time a bold stroke for theatrical realism: the convention insisted that middle-class domestic dramas had to have a happy ending cobbled up somehow, and Jones was, in his time, doing the unconventional, unacceptable thing by insisting on a rigid code of social morality which brought his story close to domestic tragedy.

In addition, the play, whatever its crudities and over-simplifications, was meant seriously and made no bones about its intentions. The author even departed from the standard practice of the day so far as to have it published in book form, with a preface, as soon as the American Copyright Act of 1891 made it feasible to do so without losing all control of American stage rights. Because of this, and Jones's insistence on the moral purpose of his play, it was often suggested in the 1890s and 1900s that he had been influenced in his choice of subject and its treatment by the example of Ibsen, and particularly of *Pillars of Society*, which was given a single matinée performance in London in 1880. Some colour might be lent to this suggestion by the fact that immediately before *Saints and Sinners* Jones had been associated with Herman in a very free and thoroughly softened adaptation of *The Doll's House*, retitled *Breaking a Butterfly* (1884). But Jones firmly maintained that Ibsen had had little or no influence on him; the observation of English life in *Saints and Sinners* came entirely from his own early life and experiences, while for the interpretation he put upon the material he was indebted above all to the social writings of Matthew Arnold.

And in this he may well have been right. Certainly, beyond a certain coincidence in the elementary subject-matter of *Saints and Sinners* and *Pillars of Society*, there is little or no relation between the two plays, and Jones seems to have learnt little or nothing from Ibsen as a theatrical technician. He may of course, as the century neared its end, have benefited somewhat from the freer climate for the theatrical discussion of social problems which the onset of Ibsenism created. But if so he did so unconsciously, and by reaction rather than directly: in 1891 he wrote angrily about the Ibsen influence as 'a school of modern realism which founded dramas on disease, ugliness and vice', and no doubt a lot of the success of his dramas was due to a feeling in the public that while they were ready for plays which treated seriously the social failings of the time, they did not want anything as uncivilly outspoken as Ibsen; Jones at least, whatever he might say or do, always wrote like a gentleman.

After *Saints and Sinners*, which despite mixed-to-hostile notices had a very fair success with the public and a more-than-respectable run, Jones wrote several deliberately light-weight plays, two of them in collaboration with Wilson Barrett, before taking up where he had left off and writing another problem play. His next serious onslaught on the playgoing public was not launched until 1889, in *Wealth* and *The Middleman*. Both deal in decidedly melodramatic terms with businessmen and their problems. *Wealth* is about a rich and successful iron-master who tries to make his only daughter marry a worthless nephew. She loves someone else, and as a result of a scene over this, caused by her cousin at a party thrown to announce their engagement, is turned out of the house by her irate father. He then, under the influence of the nephew, speculates wildly and goes conveniently mad; but when he is dying his daughter, now happily married to the man she loves, returns to receive his blessing and inherit the remains of his wealth. *The Middleman* concerns a potter obsessed with the idea of recovering the lost method of glazing perfected by old potters, and the big scene of the play shows him finally succeeding after being reduced in poverty and despair to keeping the furnace heated by burning all his possessions. The romantic sub-plot has his daughter ruined by his employer's son in the first act and happily married to him while the old man enjoys great prosperity as a result of his discovery in the last.

Wealth was widely felt to be too uncompromising in its gloom and too lacking in romance to succeed, but *The Middleman* ushered in an era of almost unbroken success for Jones. It was his next play, *Judah* (1890), however, which really confirmed his place with Pinero as the leading dramatist of his age. Its plot is relatively simple and compact: Judah, a cleric whose religious convictions verge on fanaticism, comes to love and deeply believe in Vashti, a young girl who can apparently heal people by fasting and faith. But it transpires that her gifts are all a fake, in which she has been stage-managed by her father. Judah at first tries to protect her, but at last realizes that the only way their life together can work will be if they begin again with a clean slate; the finale is a dramatic confession-scene which implies the start of a new life for Judah and his wife. Shaw, characteristically, objected to Jones that the play 'consists of clever preliminaries; and when the real play begins with the matrimonial experiment of Jonah and Vashti, down comes the curtain as usual'. Nevertheless, the play is novel in its subject-matter and unusually concentrated in its effect. It is not for nothing that Archer later found in Jones 'the first marked symptoms of a reaction – of a tendency to reject extrinsic and fanciful ornament in dialogue, and to rely for its effect upon its vivid appropriateness to character and situation'.

Of *The Dancing Girl* (1891), his next great success, there is very little to say, though at least one contemporary critic, in *The Saturday Review*, opined that in it Jones had nearly written a great play. It remains entertaining for the lunatic intricacies of its plot, which involves three principals: an extravagant and dissolute Duke; Drusilla Ives, the daughter of one of his Quaker tenants who has become the toast of London as a dancer while convincing her father that she is respectably employed as a governess; and Sybil Craig, the crippled daughter of the duke's agent. When Drusilla turns down the Duke's offer of marriage and her father, discovering her true mode of employment, breaks up a farewell party at the Duke's, Sybil prevents the Duke from poisoning himself and the happy couple are seen at the last setting earnestly about rebuilding the Duke's shattered fortunes, which have been largely squandered on Drusilla. Up to the fourth act the story at least keeps moving, but from then on all is anticlimax; whatever else the play may be, it is certainly not "well-made".

For *The Crusaders* (1891), his first venture into management, Jones turned aside from 'strong' drama into satirical comedy. The play, actually, is rather amusing: a group of reformers embark on a wholesale crusade against the abuses of modern London, only to find in the end that the only result of their efforts has been an increase to income tax of 2d. in the pound. It was also notable in its time for being presented in a set decorated entirely by William Morris, and for Jones's attempt during its run, rapidly foiled, to put an end to payment for theatre programmes by having them distributed free. But the play was not a success, and neither was his next, *The Tempter* (1893), a five-act verse tragedy about devilish intervention in human affairs set in the Middle Ages. The play remained one of Jones's own favourites, representing as it no doubt did his major attempt to produce 'real literature', but it found few other supporters; in particular Jones's blank verse came under fire, and though Shaw found it 'a model of speakability' the critical aftermath of the production involved Jones and his reviewers in a lot of rather odd squabbling about whether the use of such words as 'bedlam' and 'superior' could be sanctioned in modern blank verse, depending on whether the Elizabethans had or had not used them.

Jones's casting-about for a new outlet for his talents, begun in *The Crusaders* and *The Tempter*, led him in various directions in the next few years, with more or less success. *The Masqueraders* (1894) is a deliberately wayward and fanciful piece about one woman's relations with two men, 'a dissolute drunken waster' whom she first marries and then stays with for the sake of their child, and an impractical astronomer who having come unexpectedly into a fortune gambles his money against the woman and child on a turn of the cards. He wins, and in the end takes the heroine and her sister into his house while he tactfully sets off on an expedition to Africa. It provided George Alexander and Mrs Patrick Campbell with two showy roles, but did not carry Jones's art as a dramatist much farther, and its alleged intention to hold a mirror up to the sham of married life in high society is remote from any effect the play as written could possibly make.

With his next two notable plays, however, *The Case of Rebellious Susan* (1894) and *The Triumph of the Philistines* (1895) he put into practice Shaw's advice that he should attempt a thorough-going comedy of manners. In *The Case of Rebellious Susan* he did so with some ingenuity: plunging his audience at once into the middle of the drama with Susan's rebellion against the unfairness of a world in which a man's peccadillos can be cheerfully condoned while a woman is not permitted even the slightest, most momentary deviation from strict, conventional rectitude, it proceeds to build its comedy boldly on the working-out of her attempt to turn the tables and break this particular masculine monopoly by embarking on a short-lived affair of her own in Cairo before she returns at the last to health, home and husband. Almost too bold for Sir Charles Wyndham, who somewhat against his better judgment finally agreed to stage the play exactly as written, but not before he had fired off a volley of letters to Jones containing propositions such as this:

I stand bewildered today as ever at finding an author, a clean living, clear-minded man, hoping to extract laughter from an audience on the score of a woman's impurity. I can realize the picture of a bad woman and her natural and desirable end being portrayed, but that amusement pure and simple should be expected from the sacrifice of that one indispensable quality in respect for womanhood astounds me.

Despite which, and despite generally unfavourable notices, the play went on to be a considerable box-office success. *The*

43

Triumph of the Philistines did much less well; its attack on the prudery and hypocrisy of the average Englishman faced with anything resembling bohemianism in behaviour was found altogether too broad and uncompromising, and though Shaw thought the play one of Jones's better works Jones himself later acknowledged that he had never managed to order his materials in the piece quite rightly for the maximum effect. Certainly the love-relationship beset with misunderstandings which provides the central thread of the play is too cavalierly plonked down in front of us as an achieved fact for us to be involved very deeply in its subsequent ups and downs.

Nothing daunted, Jones next presented the biggest failure of all his mature plays, and his own dearest favourite, *Michael and His Lost Angel* (1896). The play is a 'strong' drama about a battle for supremacy between Michael Faversham, a man of strong religious convictions, and Audrie Lesden, an unhappily married free soul with whom he falls passionately in love. Under the stress of emotion, and exceptional circumstances, he gives way to his desires momentarily, but then he repents, enforces a separation, and finds some sort of consolation in his conversion to Roman Catholicism. But Audrie does not repent, even at the end, when she is dying and lets herself go so far, for Michael, as to pay some lip-service to the concept of a sin she has no real awareness of having committed.

Perhaps because the play did fail so disastrously, it has nearly always found critics to say much in its favour, and even those who are sharpest in their strictures on its short-comings in character-drawing (especially of Michael, who is by any standards a very dull and unappealing creation) come round one way or another to accepting that *Michael and His Lost Angel* is in some mysterious fashion Jones's most substantial and serious achievement. Unfortunately it is not that, not by a long way. As so often, only the coolly professional Archer saw what is really wrong with it: given that the play is essentially a duologue between Michael and Audrie, faith and paganism, it is necessary that after paganism has won its brief victory Audrie should do all in her power to consolidate her position, 'to break down in theory the ascetic ideal which has collapsed in practice.' But no, instead of the necessary confrontation, the battle of wills which Audrie must engage in even if she is ultimately defeated, the play trails off into irrelevant side issues, and so remains both structurally and emotionally deficient.

Two more minor works, *The Rogue's Comedy* and *The Physician*, and then, at the turn of the century, Jones was at last ready to produce his two best plays, *The Liars* (1897) and *Mrs Dane's Defence* (1900). One is a comedy, the other is a drama with an unhappy ending. Both show him in complete command of the technique of the English well-made play, the immaculately neat and workmanlike, economically and not too obtrusively constructed drama of contemporary social life. And both, ironically enough, show that even as he exercised his talents in this direction with total ease and unselfconsciousness, the forces which were to destroy the well-made play as a vehicle for domestic tragedy or tragi-comedy were already at work in him.

Particularly in the second. *The Liars* stays firmly on the side of comedy: a comedy of intrigue and sentiment which owes something to Sheridan and perhaps something more to the, at that time unmentionable, example of Oscar Wilde. The liars of the title (which was, incredibly, found by several critics at the time to be offensively outspoken) are society at large, but more specifically the group of friends who try to help the heroine, Lady Jessica Nepean, to escape her extravagantly jealous husband's suspicions over an escapade which was in itself entirely innocent and harmless. Much of the fun in the play comes from the frantic attempts of all and sundry to keep a consistent line in the ever-complicating tangle of lies and half-truths which, instead of holding jealousy at bay, draws the suspicious husband deeper and deeper into its web. Finally it is all too much, and Falkner, Lady Jessica's would-be suitor, is at last driven by Nepean's complete unreasonableness to tell him the simple truth and plan an elopement with Lady Jessica. This, however, is prevented at the eleventh hour by the arguments of a bystander, Sir Christopher Dering, who brings things down to earth again and reunites husband and wife.

All of this is light and charming, turning the materials of melodrama consistently to the uses of comedy. There may be disagreements about the charms of Lady Jessica herself, whom Archer found 'an empty-headed, empty-hearted creature', and certainly Sir Christopher's great set speech in the last act is rather too much of a good thing for modern audiences. But all in all *The Liars* remains a charming, expert comedy which would probably bear revival very well.

Mrs Dane's Defence demonstrably does bear revival; it has become one of the classics of English well-made drama. And yet, while of a piece with the most solid conservative drama of the 1890s, it does contain, especially in its later stages, a number of curious undertones which suggest something of what was to come and herald the end of the whole structure of social convention which made the well-made play possible. It is therefore worth looking at the play in some detail.

We begin with a succession of conversations in the drawing-room at Lady Eastney's country home during a smart soirée. From them we learn that Mrs Dane is a charming, mysterious woman who has lately settled in the village; that a young man has at first claimed to recognize her as a Miss Felicia Hindemarsh who was some years before involved in an unsavoury episode abroad, then taken it back; that his aunt, from sheer ill-nature and jealousy, is determined nevertheless to believe the story and put it about; and that Mrs Dane and a handsome young man, Lionel Cartaret, are in love and will marry if Lionel's guardian Sir Daniel Cartaret, a famous judge, will approve the match.

The second act shows the growth of the scandal. It has got to the point where Mrs Dane cannot ignore it, and neither can Lionel or Sir Daniel. She is urged to defend herself, and manages for the moment to do so, with letters from the original source of the story reiterating his subsequent retraction, and by bribing a private detective hired by her arch-enemy Mrs Bulson-Porter to say that he could find no evidence that she and Miss Hindemarsh are one and the same.

But the plot is thickening. In the third act, Sir Daniel has reached the point of accepting the truth of her story, based closely on the actual life-history of a dead cousin whose name she has taken. But inconvenient evidence is piling up against her, and finally a slip of the tongue arouses Sir Daniel's suspicions to such an extent that by slow cross-examination he at last manages to get the truth out of her.

In the fourth act matters are finally resolved. Lady Eastney, for her own satisfaction, insists that Sir Daniel must not let Mrs Bulson-Porter get away without signing a written apology to Mrs Dane. Lionel, even knowing the truth about Mrs Dane, is desperate enough to run off with her anyway, but is dissuaded by his uncle. Mrs Dane is likewise persuaded to see the necessity of her sacrificing Lionel for his own good, and goes off to leave Sir Daniel and Lady Eastney at last on the brink of matrimony, with a hint of future romance between Lionel and Lady Eastney's niece Janet Colquhoun.

So far, so good. The plot is impeccably put together, so that even the most doubtful points – about Mrs Dane's changing stories of her early life, for instance – are readily explicable in terms of her rather weak and vacillating character. The last act, certainly, is something of a novelty in the genre in that instead of bringing things at once to a slap-bang conclusion right after the big interrogation scene and ultimate breakdown of Mrs Dane, Jones allows a played-down conclusion coming to a dying fall as Mrs Dane quietly walks out into the night.

But let us examine more closely the precise way that final turn of events is reached. When Sir Daniel first proposes to take Mrs Dane's case in hand and get at the truth he puts a simple alternative to his ward: if he finds her guiltless Lionel and she can marry at once; on the other hand, if she is in fact the guilty woman she is said to be, then Lionel must break off all communication with her immediately. To which Lionel's reply is 'Of course, sir'. The whole basis of the British well-made play is summed up in those three words. As long as the convention of social behaviour is observed whereby a woman who is not, as they would say, pure has no right to exist, must instantly be shunned by all, and could not in any conceivable circumstances be married by a man of honour, then the plays work. Equally, if Lionel were to say, or even to think, at that juncture 'I don't give a damn who or what she has been. I want her and I love her', then the play would instantly fall apart.

This way of falling-apart, the fate which was to overtake the well-made social drama early in the 1900s under the onslaught of Shaw and the New Drama generally, but also by more insidious influences in a world of changing social and moral standards, is however strongly prefigured in the final scene, when the crisis is over and all that is left for the characters to do is to decide how they will continue living from then on. For the scene is full of ironies and ambiguities which can hardly be anything but intentional. They are introduced by Lady Eastney, Mrs Dane's steadfast friend and supporter, who suddenly begins a disquisition on the unfairness of it all, and leaves a doubt hanging in the air about whether, despite Sir Daniel's protestations, the difference between a virtuous and a fallen woman is quite so clear-cut as society supposes.

Next comes the scene in which Sir Daniel sets about reasoning Lionel out of going away with Mrs Dane. This he does by a number of half-truths and at least one bare-faced lie, which the audience must immediately recognize as such. He points out that Lionel will never be able to forgive and forget that she has loved and given herself to another man first (though he himself is on the point of marrying a widow), and that her child by this other man will be a constant blot on their happiness (though he himself has adopted most satisfactorily the son borne by the women he loved to another man). Does the presence of a legal contract in each case really make so much difference; can Sir Daniel, in fact, or the author, or his audience, believe that it makes *all* the difference? Then again Sir Daniel claims kinship with Lionel in his grief because he too had determined to give up the women he loved, through the promptings of duty and so that no shame should attach to the names of either. 'I am not asking you to do anything I have not done.' But we know from what he has said earlier that this is a direct lie: he did not so decide, but was left by his beloved, Lionel's mother, for the highest of motives, and he has already confessed to Lady Eastney that he would gladly give up every success he has since achieved just to be waiting for her again on the platform and know she would come.

And there is more. When Sir Daniel turns his attention to Mrs Dane he is equally disingenuous, painting with lawyerly skill a picture of her life with Lionel, them both rendered social outcasts when the story comes out, as come out it must. But of course he knows and we know that it mustn't; it couldn't, hushed up and covered by a signed apology as it is. She might well make Lionel an excellent wife, and we cannot help feeling that she is in fact much nearer the truth when she retorts bitterly that evidently her main sin is the really unforgivable one of being found out. But what would come of well-made social drama in a world where right and wrong were not as distinct as black and white, and where the only criterion was what you could get away with – especially as the margin of what you could get away with grew yearly wider?

What indeed. Certainly Henry Arthur Jones never found out, and having got so far as to pose the question in *Mrs Dane's Defence* he rapidly withdrew into more comfortable territory. During the remaining 24 years of his life he wrote some 26 full-length plays, of which 16 were produced in London or New York, and two more filmed but never staged. He came increasingly to be regarded as a back number, was beset by money troubles, and latterly deserted the stage more and more for political pamphleteering. Two at least of his later comedies, *Whitewashing Julia* (1903) and *Dolly Reforming Herself* (1908) had a deserved success: the former is a lighthearted reworking of the theme of *Mrs Dane's Defence* – was or was not Mrs Julia Wren, attractive and mysterious newcomer in an English village, once morganatically married to the Duke of Savona? – with this time no definite explanation one way or the other and a happy ending for all concerned. The theme of *Dolly Reforming Herself* is indicated by the quotation from Voltaire Jones used as an epigraph on the privately printed edition: 'Mennon conçut le projet un jour d'être parfaitement sage. Il n'y a guère d'homme à qui cette folie n'est pas quelquefois passée par la tête.' A husband battles endlessly, ingeniously and in vain to keep the expenditure of his extravagant wife within reasonable bounds, while she guilefully does all she can to out-wit him.

Then in 1923, unexpectedly, the old dramatist found himself author of a major West End success: his drama *The Lie*, written and performed in New York nine years earlier, was given its first London production as a vehicle for Sybil Thorndike. It was a melodramatic tale of two sisters, both in love with the same man. One of them has had an illegitimate baby, but she lets the man believe the other is in fact the child's mother, and marries him before he can find out the truth, leaving her sister merely the consolation of her love for the child. Jones seemed like – was – a figure from the past, but audiences happily gobbled up what he set before them. By now, though, he had finally given up writing for the stage, and he produced nothing more before his death in 1929. He continued going to the theatre almost up to his death, and in 1925 was was to be found testily taking Pirandello to task for his failure to provide *Right You Are if You Think So* with a proper dénouement.

He had, of course, his own ideas of craftsmanship, and these were far from Pirandello's. They were, in essence, very much the same as Sardou's, the only vital difference being in the sort of material to which they were applied. Even Shaw, a friend of Jones's but an implacable enemy of Sardoodledum, recognized Jones's mastery of theatrical craft as complete, starting his notice of *Michael and His Lost Angel* in the *Saturday Review* by remarking:

> One of the greatest comforts in criticising the work of Mr Henry Arthur Jones is that the critic can go straight to the subject-matter without troubling about the dramatic con-struction. In the born writer the style is the man; and with the born dramatist, the play is the subject. Mr Jones's plays grow; they are not cut out of bits of paper and stuck to-gether . . .

And Jones himself always emphasized the important part that sheer instinct played in his writing. In answer to a question from Archibald Henderson in 1923 he explained how 'some-times a succession of incidents may *dart simultaneously* into the brain', instancing the third act of *The Liars*, seemingly one of his most intricate pieces of plot manipulation, which, he said 'came to me, not as a sequence of situations, but at one glance, as one sees a landscape, foreground and middle distance and background all at once.'

This is no doubt true, and yet in an important sense it is irrelevant: for all his interest in raising popular theatre to the condition of literature again, Henry Arthur Jones was always, when most successful, a man of the theatre first and foremost, so thoroughly conversant with every trick of the dramatist's trade that he could afford to trust himself largely to instinct in the first vital stages of creation, no matter how much hard work might be involved in 'compelling the scheme to go on all fours.' Less sophisticated and in many ways less intelligent than Pinero, he yet did almost as much as Pinero to bring the English well-made play to its short dramatic maturity, and in *Mrs Dane's Defence* wrote a play as likely as any of its time to last.

Arthur Wing Pinero

With the career of Sir Arthur Wing Pinero (1855–1934) we come to the high point of the well-made play's career in Britain. Not a very high point, it has been usual to say for the last fifty years or so. And yet, whatever else may be said of him, Pinero is a dramatist whose best plays – half a dozen or so, and not just one or two – remain constantly revivable and find new audiences in each generation. Moreover, he was the only British dramatist who consistently managed to make the well-made play work, not only on its first audiences but on succeeding generations, and not only in farce, where well-madeness is necessary, and comedy, where it is desirable, but in serious drama – precisely the type of play generally supposed most capable of standing on its own legs without the adventitious aids of mere technique, and most liable to be vitiated by the failure in sincerity which is, to our incorrigibly romantic English minds, always felt to be somehow implied by a clear knowledge of what one is doing before and while one is doing it.

Like Scribe – and many more respectable dramatists – Pinero was already an experienced man of the theatre before he wrote his first play. He was an inveterate theatre-goer from his early teens, a professional actor by the age of nineteen, and a performed dramatist by the age of twenty-two, when his first piece to be played in London, *£200 a Year*, was done as a benefit. Two other one-act plays were put on by Irving at the Lyceum, where Pinero was working as an actor, and in 1880 Pinero's first full-length play, *The Money-Spinner*, had a modest success. A number of other plays followed in rapid succession, the only one of even slight interest being *The Squire* (1881), until in 1885 he achieved his first major success with a farce, *The*

Magistrate, in which he first achieved dramatic maturity and wrote a play which bears revival. In 1888 he flirted with sentiment in *Sweet Lavender* and in 1889 wrote his first attempt at 'strong' controversial drama in *The Profligate*. From this time on he concentrated more and more on drama, and in this genre had a string of almost uninterrupted successes until *Mid-Channel* (1909). Thereafter he continued writing plays, on and off, but none of them had any noticeable success at the time and none is remembered now except perhaps *The Enchanted Cottage* (1922), which achieved some of the popularity denied it on stage when it was filmed in the 1940s.

So Pinero's effective career as a dramatist lasted about a quarter of a century, and during that time he wrote some score of plays, among which three farces and three dramas or dramatic comedies have been regularly revived, and two or three more would probably bear reviving if anyone thought to do so. He had – we may as well concede it at the outset – no 'philosophy of life', no message that he was burning to deliver to the public, no deep-rooted personal obsessions which had willy nilly to find expression. He was a professional writer who took his profession seriously, and his plays, where they triumph, are above all a triumph of craftsmanship. Not just craftsmanship, of course: that could hardly keep his plays alive for more than fifty years. He had ideas too: not so much ideas about life, but ideas for subjects which would make interesting plays. He was, for what it is worth – and that is not a little – a writer who could tell interesting stories to maximum effect on the stage. Many, setting out to do much more, have succeeded in doing much less.

I would not like to be misunderstood. All this is true, and yet it should not be taken to imply that Pinero was a very self-conscious craftsman, let alone artist. Though he knew fairly well what had been and was going on in the popular French theatre – he spent quite a bit of his dramatic apprenticeship adapting 'from the French' or acting in such adaptations by other people – he seems to have spent little energy on considering exactly what he was up to as a dramatist and how his aims might best be expressed in general terms. He was a practical dramatist, he wrote plays. He relied on his instinct to show him what would and would not be effective on the stage, and if his instinct led him astray once he knew better next time.

When Archer asked him about his routine of composition he said 'Before beginning to write a play, I always make sure, by means of a definite scheme, that there is *a* way of doing it; but whether I ultimately follow that way is a totally different matter.' And later he characterized the slavish following of a drawn-up scheme as 'carpenter's work, belonging to a lower form of composition.' He firmly believed, moreover, that the only regulators of his plays' construction were the characters in them – 'The beginning of a play to me is a little world of people. I live with them, get familiar with them, and *they* tell me the story.' Which, if he was not being disingenuous – and there is no reason to suppose he was – simply shows how well he had assimilated the principles of the well-made play without even being conscious that he had done so. Certainly it is noticeable, and notable, that after that bad but interesting transitional work *The Profligate*, whenever there is an evident weakness of construction it always coincides with a weakness, a failure of confidence or courage, in the depiction of one of the characters involved.

To see exactly how Pinero worked as a craftsman, it may be useful to look first at the first-in-time of his remembered plays, the farces: as Archer said, 'let no one despise the technical lessons to be learnt from a good farce.' It might be objected that after all, farces are nothing but technique. But in fact this is not so, and particularly is it not so of Pinero's farces, chief among them *The Magistrate* (1885), *The Schoolmistress* (1886), *Dandy Dick* (1887), *The Cabinet Minister* (1890) and *The Amazons* (1893). It has often, and fairly, been said that in them Pinero created a new genre, the 'farce of character': in a sense the dictum just quoted about his drama at large can be applied to his farces as readily as to any of his work.

Unlike most writers of farces he does not stick at stereotypes for his characters – deceived husband, indiscreet wife, foolish lover, precocious schoolboy, garrulous dotard, saucy maid and a host of others who are just what their label gives them out to be and no more – and then pin everything on the dexterity with which these two-dimensional puppets are manœuvred in and out of embarrassing situations with each other. Instead, he creates characters who are, against all odds, strangely believable, idiosyncratic. Once these characters exist, they are made to act according entirely to the dictates of their own natures, the only improbability permitted being that they do so with greater abandon and lack of self-consciousness than most people in real life do most of the time.

They accept, that is, for the purposes of the play, the logic of extreme solutions, and, having decided to act, never do things by half measures. Hence the extraordinary situations into which they manœuvre themselves – and the phrase is significant: the point about Pinero is that if he is conscious of his art he is adept at concealing it, and keeping us unconscious, as we never are in Feydeau, that the dramatist is manœuvring his characters rather than merely bringing them together in such a way that everything following follows inevitably.

Thus to say that the mechanism of Pinero's farces is less consummately handled than that of Feydeau's is both true and irrelevant: they are after different things, and working in different genres. In Feydeau we are not asked to involve ourselves in any way, but simply to observe and admire the machinery. In Pinero we get rather a chain reaction, starting from one *outré* situation and the placing of a group of extraordinary but not downright unbelievable characters in it. Take *Dandy Dick* for instance: it begins in a small way with the unworldly Dean of St Marvell's, eager to raise money for the restoration of the cathedral spire, allowing himself to be persuaded by his horsey sister Georgiana Tidman (or George Tid as she is usually known) to put £50 on a horse. Once in that deep, he embarks, through a combination of innocence and enthusiasm, on a reckless progression via giving the horse some, as he thinks, healthful bolus mash to being arrested (incognito) for trying to poison the horse on the eve of the race, imprisoned in the local gaol, rescued with the connivance of the constable's wife, formerly a cook in the household, from the cart in which he is being taken to trial, and restored, shaken and somewhat humanized, to the deanery in time to witness the engagement of George Tid to Sir Tristam Marsden, joint owner of the horse Dandy Dick, and be blackmailed into taking a lenient view of the slightly too dashing exploits of his two daughters on their way to a dance they were forbidden to attend.

And what, we are bamboozled into saying by the end of the play, could be more natural than that? But then Pinero's great strength in his farces lies in arranging things so that, given the initial premise, everything seems naturally to follow on from it. *Seems*, and perhaps seemed so even to him. But of course in drama nothing really is inevitable. The mere fact that a play begins somewhere and ends somewhere imposes a basic artificiality, since nothing in life just begins and just ends. So, drama must be a constant balance, weighted one way or another, between the need for contrivance and the need to suggest that nothing has been contrived. There is no easy way out of this, least of all in drama which is in one respect or another deliberately designed to seem realistic.

With Pinero, as with all those who subscribe somehow to the theory of the well-made play, the issue is simply stated: how to convey the appearance, the impression of real life unmanipulated, while at the same time manipulating it as much as one needs to fit into a play which keeps the audience held unquestioning as long, at least, as the play lasts? 'Willing suspension of disbelief' is a phrase much bandied about in this context, but it is a misnomer. No one ever willingly suspended disbelief, or could if he would. Audiences have to be made to suspend disbelief, and on the degree to which Pinero succeeds in making his audiences follow him and his stories without question depends his lasting effectiveness as a dramatist.

As to the difficulty of doing so, we can judge only by results. In comedy, it would seem, it must be relatively easy to keep one's audience believing even while writing in an unmistakeably artificial form. Obviously it is not true that so long as you mean to be funny anything goes, as many aspiring humorists have found to their cost. But it does seem that even if obvious devices like extravagant inconsistencies of character, incredibly neat coincidences and the like are as little acceptable in the central matter of comedy as they are in the central matter of drama, we are willing to take a more charitable view of such evident contrivance on the margins of comedy, and even find positive pleasure in the preternatural neatness with which the pieces of comedy are finally made to fit together. Not so in drama, and to this extent at least Pinero's successful experience on the lighter side of the well-made play need not be a help and might prove a positive hindrance when it came to applying his talents to straight drama.

Certainly it might have seemed that this was the case from his first thorough-going drama, *The Profligate*. This was not, as it happens, his first flirtation with the stuff of drama, but before in his early plays *The Money-Spinner* and *The Squire*, and later in *Sweet Lavender* (1888) and *The Weaker Sex* (1889), he had chosen to treat potentially dramatic, even tragic materials from the comic point of view, and water them down with easy sentimentalism. *The Money-Spinner* is a silly story about a wife who, having conveniently been brought up in a gaming-house, manages to get her husband out of financial difficulties by cheating at cards, and talk the amiable ninny who has been cheated into accepting and even liking the situation. But at least it is consistently light and drama is held effectively at bay.

The Squire is quite another matter. Pinero showed Hamilton Fyfe the note upon which the play was based. It ran 'The notion of a young couple secretly married – the girl about to become a mother – finding that a former wife is still in existence. The heroine amongst those who respect and love her. The fury of a rejected lover who believes her to be a guilty woman. Two men face to face at night-time. Query – kill the first wife?' It sounds like the plot of a raging melodrama, but in the event Pinero treated it as drama (unlikely drama, granted) and then, having set up the 'strong' situation, allowed it to fritter away both by failing to construct the intrigue further (nothing more really happens until the first wife dies improbably but con- veniently to make way for a happy ending) and, moreover, allowing all his characters, but especially the husband, to act with the wildest lack of consistency or even comprehensible motive betweenwhiles. Despite which, Archer was already moved, on the strength of this play, to describe Pinero in 1882 as 'a thoughtful and conscientious writer with artistic aims, if not yet with full command of his artistic means', and predict an honourable future for him.

We need not waste time on *Sweet Lavender*, an ably concocted weepie with no noticeable claims to sense, or *The Weaker Sex*, a scarcely less silly tale about a mother and daughter in love with the same man. Let us move instead to *The Profligate*, which, whatever its faults as drama – and they are many – does at least mark a clear turning-point in Pinero's career. Up to 1889 he had been known as a writer of farces and soap-opera, that is, an eminently respectable, uncontroversial sort of dramatist. *The Profligate* changed all that, and for this reason if no other it is worthy of study.

It must be said to start with, though, that in most respects it is a thoroughly bad play. Briefly, this is the plot. Dunstan Renshaw is about to marry Leslie Brudenhall, ward of a solicitor, and is to meet her at the solicitor's office, just round the corner from the registry office. He arrives first, with a hangover, meets there an old friend of his who happens to drop in, to whom he can conveniently relate the story of his courtship. Meanwhile it transpires that Leslie's guardian's partner, Murray, has also fallen in love with her, too late, and is unhappy about the match. After the couple have gone another young woman, Janet Preece, arrives, recommended by the bride's brother, and enlists Murray's aid in tracing a libertine who did her wrong; Murray recognizes him as Renshaw, under an assumed name. In the second act Janet turns up, quite by chance, at the Florentine villa where Renshaw and Leslie are honeymooning; one way and another all is revealed. Finally Renshaw resolves the situation by taking poison; or at least he does in the printed text, but for the first production Pinero was prevailed upon to permit a reconciliation between him and Leslie, and a sort of happy ending.

Now the first thing to occur to one about this is that the story could not possibly as it stands make a well-made play in any sense of the term. The mechanism of the exposition (convenient appearance of a confidant for Renshaw, soliloquies to put us in the picture about Murray's feelings) is extremely cumbersome, the appearance of Janet in the same office, though heavily planted, stretches our credulity a bit, and the only pointer forward (apart from a vague supposition on the audience's part, not to be relied on very far, that where there is a secret it must sooner or later be revealed) is the question of what Murray, the one outsider in full possession of the facts, will do with them. But this proves a false pointer, since in the event he does nothing, and the author has to begin all over again in the second act, with a coincidence – that Janet should turn up absolutely by chance in the one place in the world where she is virtually certain to run into Renshaw again – so extravagant that no audience in its right mind is likely to swallow it with ease.

It is possible to think up half a dozen ways by which the means of the revelation could have been planted in the first act, to keep the audience in proper suspense, but Pinero adopted none of them, and his play therefore lacks any of the advantages, however superficial we may judge them to be, which well-madeness à la Scribe would confer. On the other hand, it certainly does not have any other advantages to snatch a grace beyond the reach of art. The dialogue throughout is on the level of Murray's ultimatum to Renshaw:

> For the sake of one poor creature, your wife, I have been dishonest to another poor creature, your broken plaything! For one month I have lied for you in act and in spirit. In the race between you and your victim I have given the strong man a month's start; to her a month of suspense, to you a month of thoughtless happiness. You have taken it, enjoyed it, steeped yourself to the lips in it; and now, from this day, you play the game of your life without a confederate. Our paths divide!

And in any case everyone in sight acts with such wild inconsistency, even according to the play's own implicit standards, that the question, much debated at the time, of which ending is the right one, seems entirely beside the point: if Renshaw is not the man to kill himself, he is not either the man to take his own infatuation with Leslie so seriously, or she, alternatively, the woman to forgive and at least try to forget. In any case, the whole problem belongs, as here presented, to a sort of senti-mental Victorian dream-world – as Pinero himself later realized, if we are to believe the evidence of how he treated a similar subject ten years later in *The Gay Lord Quex* (1899).

And yet this silly, badly constructed play had its measure of success, if only *de scandale*, and established Pinero as the fore-most serious dramatist of his generation in Britain. That this judgement, though hasty, might after all be correct his next serious drama, *The Second Mrs Tanqueray* (1893) went a long way towards proving. The play was so famous in its day, and re-mains still so very much the play above all others with which Pinero's name is immediately associated, that it is difficult to approach it with an open mind and try to appreciate it for what it is. Of course it is not quite so good as some of its most extravagant early supporters thought it – though it never was accepted without question as a masterpiece – and it is not so bad as some of its more determined detractors, then and since, have maintained it to be. That goes almost without saying.

But where along this scale should our judgement place it? On the whole, I would say, much nearer the top than the bot-tom. Its very end is highly arguable – it is far too convenient that Paula Tanqueray should kill herself off so readily, and she does not strike us previously as being the sort of woman who would do so, nor does the dramatist make any apparent attempt to suggest to us that she might – but up to that point it is almost a model of what the well-made play at its best may do. The question at issue is how far one thinks this best is good enough, how far the end justifies the means.

As it happens, the very first scene, the exposition, brings two of the most vocal contemporary commentators into direct collision. Here is Archer on it:

> *The Second Mrs Tanqueray* requires an unusual amount
> of preliminary retrospect. We have to learn the history of

Aubrey Tanqueray's first marriage, with the mother of Ellean, as well the history of Paula Ray's past life. The mechanism employed to this end has been much criticized, but seems to me admirable. Aubrey gives a farewell dinner-party to his intimate friends, Misquith and Jayne. Cayley Drummle, too, is expected, but has not arrived when the play opens. Without naming the lady, Aubrey announces to his guests his approaching marriage. He proposes to go out with them, and has one or two notes to write before doing so. Moreover, he is not sorry to give them an opportunity to talk over the announcement he has made; so he retires to a side-table in the same room, to do his writing. Misquith and Jayne exchange a few speeches in an undertone, and then Cayley Drummle comes in, bringing the story of George Orreyd's marriage to the unmentionable Miss Hervey. This story is so unpleasant to Tanqueray that, to get out of the conversation, he returns to his writing; but still he cannot help listening to Cayley's comments on George Orreyd's 'disappearance'; and at last the situation becomes so intolerable to him that he purposely leaves the room, bidding the other two 'Tell Cayley the news.' The technical manipulation of all this seems to me above reproach – dramatically effective and yet life-like in every detail. If one were bound to raise an objection, it would be to the coincidence which brings to Cayley's knowledge, on one and the same evening, two such exactly similar misalliances in his own circle of acquaintance. But these are just the coincidences that do constantly happen. Every one knows that life is full of them.

The exposition might, no doubt, have been more eco-nomically effected. Cayley Drummle might have figured as sole confidant and chorus; or even he might have been dis-pensed with, and all that was necessary might have appeared in colloquies between Aubrey and Paula on the one hand, Aubrey and Ellean on the other. But Cayley as sole confidant – the 'Charles, his friend,' of eighteenth-century comedy – would have been more plainly conventional than Cayley as one of a trio of Aubrey's old cronies, representing the society he is sacrificing in entering upon this experimental marriage; and to have conveyed the necessary information without any confidant or chorus at all would (one fancies) have strained probability, or, still worse, impaired consistency of character. Aubrey could not naturally discuss his late wife either with her successor or with her daughter; while, as for Paula's past, all he wanted was to avert his eyes from it. I do not say that these difficulties might not have been overcome; for, in the vocabulary of the truly ingenious dramatist there is no such word as impossible. But I do suggest that the result would scarcely have been worth the trouble, and that it is hypercriticism which objects to an exposition so natural and probable as that of *The Second Mrs Tanqueray*, simply on the ground that certain characters are introduced for the purpose of conveying certain information. It would be foolish to expect of every work of art an absolutely austere economy of means.

Shaw, it is not surprising to learn, took a very different view. Writing of the play at the time of its first production (Archer was writing nearly twenty years after the event) Shaw said:

> When one notes the naive machinery of the exposition of the first act, in which two whole actors are wasted on sham parts, and the hero, at his own dinner party, is compelled to get up and go ignominiously into the next room 'to write some letters' when something has to be said behind his back; when one follows Cayley Drummle, the confidant to whom both Paula and her husband explain themselves, for the benefit of the audience; when one counts the number of doors which Mr Pinero needs to get his characters on and off stage, and how they have finally to be supplemented by the inevitable 'French windows' (two of them); and when the activity of the postman is taken into consideration, it is impossible to avoid the conclusion that what most of our critics mean by mastery of stagecraft is recklessness in the substitution of dead machinery and lay figures for vital action and real characters.

Which is right? Why, both of course, or neither. Shaw is pointing out the artifice by which Pinero gets his effects and makes his points; for him it is wrong in itself. Archer is examining the artifice, and saying that it justifies itself because it works. Shaw does not suggest any way that the necessary information could be conveyed with more economy and naturalness, or seeming naturalness, but then that is not his brief – he is more concerned with castigating the whole kind of play Pinero writes, and incidentally advocating, among others, the type of play he himself would write. Archer, on the other hand, writes as a critic of what is rather than a theorist about what might or a moralist on the subject of what ought to be. And as such, at least, his view may be accepted as the more disinterested of the two. For after all, whichever way you look at it, the exposition of *The Second Mrs Tanqueray* does work: it tells us what we have to know easily and unobtrusively, gives us a clear picture of the characters of Tanqueray and Cayley Drummle, and does not strain our credulity or insult our intelligence in the process.

The plot which follows this exposition is laid out with exemplary directness and precision, and no noticeable fumbling anywhere along the line. Among the information conveyed in the opening scene is that Ellean, the daughter of Tanqueray and his coldly correct first wife, is about to enter a convent, and the pointer at the end of the first act is a letter which arrives explaining that she has changed her mind, and intends to return and live with her father and his new wife. Obviously this whets the audience's interest to know how the convent-bred Ellean and Paula Tanqueray, whose life hitherto has been anything but sheltered, will get on.

The second act provides an answer to that question, and raises more: Paula is bored with country life and irritated because her dreams of social acceptance and new respectability have not been realized. Moreover, she is jealous of Ellean's place in Tanqueray's affections, and upset because she cannot win any affection from Ellean herself. Tanqueray for his part is worried about the effect Paula's free conversation may have on Ellean, and things come to a head when Paula accuses Tanqueray of deliberately plotting to separate her from Ellean by sending Ellean away with a neighbour, and in retaliation invites the Orreyds, the unreceivable couple we heard about in the first act, to stay.

In the third act it at once appears that the Tanquerays cannot now stand the Orreyds, who are staying. Also, Paula has been keeping from Tanqueray the letters sent to him by Ellean and the friends with whom she is travelling. No sooner has she confessed to this deception than the travellers return. Ellean has met and fallen in love with a young army officer and wants to marry him. But when he is brought in, it turns out, of course, that he is a former lover of Paula's. The way is ready for the dénouement. Paula decides that come what may, Tanqueray must know the truth. He is told, agrees to tell Ellean that for reasons he cannot disclose he must forbid Ellean's marriage. Ellean sees that Paula is the only one who can have provided the reasons, and putting two and two together guesses what they are. Paula brushes aside Tanqueray's hopeful reflections on the new start they can make, and takes poison.

The merits and demerits of this as a piece of dramatic plotting should be evident even from such a bald summary. Up to the confrontation of Paula and her ex-lover Ardale the play is as immaculate a piece of plotting as one could wish: each point is made in its proper place, each hint of trouble to come is dropped with just the right weight, each question in the audience's mind is fairly posed and fairly answered, the links in the chain are all closed and solid. The play even lives up to Pinero's own description, a story told to him by the characters. But of course character *is* construction and construction character, or at least they must seem to be so; as soon as we start to question whether a character would act this way or say that, well-madeness goes by the board.

And the first thing which strikes us about the final stages of *The Second Mrs Tanqueray*, the immediate reason why they fail to carry conviction, is that Paula acts in them inconsistently with what we know of her before. When she meets Ardale again her reaction is highly improbable: she is, as we have often been told, a woman of the world, and there is no reason why she should imagine that the mere fact he has had an affair with an older woman means that he cannot be a good husband to an innocent young girl: on the contrary, she must know that this is not necessarily so. Equally, whatever we may believe about her from what has gone before, we cannot think her likely to commit suicide, and so this last act of hers can be seen only as a rather crude device to bring about an edifying curtain. In both cases, in fact, we cannot avoid seeing the dead hand of Victorian convention at work: Pinero might decide to be bold in his choice of subject, but he held back from being too bold in the details of its ultimate working out.

And yet, paradoxically, there is something rather honest and even appealing about his patent failure to make the best of this bad job. For let us agree that dramatic characters are made, not given, and that within reason anyone can do anything: the dramatist's job is to arrange things in such a way that his characters seem likely to do what he wants them to do, and preferably more likely to do that than anything else. Considered in this light, the problems of Pinero's last act here are not insuperable. The suicide would have to go, but Paula could make an almost equally edifying end just by leaving a marriage she believed could never work and disappearing from all their lives.

As to the penultimate turn of events, that could be sorted out in various ways. If Pinero really wanted Paula to act as she does, he could prepare us earlier by leading us to believe that Paula, like many a reformed rake, has become in reaction more puritanical and correct than anyone who has lived a life of untarnished virtue. He could, but he does not. Equally, if Paula had to be responsible for the revelation, he could make her do it out of at least suppressed jealousy of Ellean, who has now stolen the affections not only of her husband but of her last lover as well. Again, Ardale could be the one responsible for their making a clean breast of it, or the revelation could come from some outside agency, or even be circumvented altogether if Tanqueray, who after all has married Paula with his eyes open and pretty fully informed about her past life, were to recognize at once the nature of the relationship between his wife and his prospective son-in-law – perhaps by way of the letter detailing her past which Paula has given him, before their wedding, and which as the play stands he has burnt unread.

All these are possibilities, and it seems unlikely Pinero did not consider them. Yet he chose to stay entirely true to his initial conception for three acts and then capitulate in the fourth, with hardly a show of smoothing things over to accommodate the weakness of the time for extraneous moralizing; it is as though he deliberately decided to let Paula be entirely true to herself for as long as possible, and then let the play go hang, rather than to tone everything down in such a way as to let the whole action lead credibly to a weak and watery ending.

That Pinero could have so modified his play had he wished I have no doubt. That, not doing so, he failed also to carry the play to its logical conclusion is no doubt a criticism of him personally, for lacking boldness, but it is not really, as it is usually supposed to be, a criticism of the 'well-made' convention in which he was working. For obviously if he had had the courage to follow his first thought through, the play would have been better made, not worse: in particular if the unfortunate revelation of Paula's former relations with Ardale came from some outside agency of which the audience but neither of the two principals involved is already aware, the linkage would be stronger and, by way of an ironic reversal, more telling than it can possibly be by an unmotivated, unprepared and highly unlikely change of heart on Paula's part.

This may seem to be labouring an obvious point unnecessarily, but proper understanding of how far *The Second Mrs Tanqueray* succeeds, and exactly where and why it fails, is vital to any serious consideration of Pinero as a dramatist. Though the play can be faulted in many ways, it still shows an enormous advance from *The Profligate*: to read the easy natural dialogue of the first three acts, for instance, after the stilted would-be literary dialogue attributed to the characters in *The Profligate*, makes it almost impossible to believe that a mere four years separate the two plays. What, one may wonder, had happened in between?

Well, for one thing, and most importantly, Ibsen had happened. When *The Doll's House* was first performed in London in 1889 its appeal had been to only a small minority of forward-looking intellectuals, and it had been damned by the critics at large. In 1891, however, Shaw's book *The Quintessence of Ibsenism* appeared, and *Ghosts, Rosmersholm* and *Hedda Gabler* followed each other in rapid succession across the London stage. The critics were still generally hostile – hysterically so in some cases – but Ibsen had at last arrived with the public at large: whatever the commercial success of his plays, they were the great talking-point of the London season. Whether Pinero liked Ibsen's plays is not at issue – certainly his own view of life, so far as it has been recorded, seems to have been thoroughly conservative, and in the realm of ideas he can have had little sympathy with most of what Ibsen stood for. But he was not unacquainted with the realities of life, and in his farces he had already suggested (under the licence accorded someone whose avowed aim is just to make us laugh) the existence of attitudes of mind and forms of behaviour far removed from the simpering conventionalities of right-thinking drama.

The Dean's daughters Salome and Sheba in *Dandy Dick*, for instance, or the boys and girls in *The Schoolmistress*, though presented in such a way that they may be accepted as fantasy, are in fact far more believable, realistic depictions of what real young people of their day must have been than any of their cardboard equivalents in contemporary 'serious' drama. Whatever Pinero's view of the ideas in Ibsen's dramas, it is readily understandable that he saw the Ibsen vogue as a clear signal that an enterprising British dramatist might, if he wished, attempt to bring some of this same human reality into straight drama as well as farce; and if *The Second Mrs Tanqueray* is seen only as the first, wavering step in that direction, it is a step none the less.

Nor, though it remained Pinero's biggest and most sensational success, was it his last step. In the particular line of drama it established it led on to *The Notorious Mrs Ebbsmith* (1895), *Iris* (1901), *His House in Order* (1906), which though described by its author as a 'comedy' is really a drama, his best, which happens to come to a happy ending, and *Mid-Channel* (1909). Each of these represents in some respect an improvement on *The Second Mrs Tanqueray*, even if only *His House in Order* is better than it as a whole. The merits and defects of *The Notorious Mrs Ebbsmith*, for instance, correspond very closely with those of *The Second Mrs Tanqueray*, except that the characters and events in which they are involved up to the unsatisfactory last act are more interesting and original than in the earlier play, and the let-down when it comes consequently even more disturbing.

This time the heroine is that exciting phenomenon, a New Woman. Agnes Ebbsmith, according to her own account (the exposition is delivered directly and quite believably to a shocked clergyman's sister who requires her to explain herself) is the daughter of a demagogue. He was unhappily married, and she swore as a child that she would at all costs avoid such a mistake, only to fall hopelessly at nineteen for a man who, once married to her, proceeded to turn into the worst kind of Victorian husband and make her life miserable for eight years. Him dead, she went round crusading for women's rights, took up nursing, and fell in with Lucas Cleeve, an unhappily married young politician whom she nursed to health and with whom she now lives in Venice in what she hopes to be a friendly platonic comradeship.

Lucas, unfortunately, does not see it this way, but wants her to dwindle into a woman again – to signify which he has bought her a very feminine, décolletée evening dress which she will not wear. Lucas's uncle, the Duke of St Olpherts, arrives in Venice to find exactly how matters stand, and proceeds to tell her the truth about Lucas, a self-indulgent weakling who cannot begin to appreciate or understand her. Agnes has unwillingly to recognize that this has elements of truth, but also she has to admit to herself that all the same she is in love with him, and when it comes to a choice between her principles and her emotions she must choose to follow her emotions and take her chance: she puts on the dress. All this, of course, on the assumption that whatever Lucas's faults and limitations, at least for the moment he loves her much as she loves him.

So far, so good. Agnes in particular is a character at once complex and believable, one of the best women characters Pinero ever wrote. But what next? Clearly, Agnes must be, and will be, disabused of her illusions about Lucas's love for her: this she is by trying on him, experimentally, the suggestion that she should settle down to a discreet position as his common mistress in London while he takes up his career again, and seeing him jump at it. But what will happen then? What does happen in the play is so ludicrously inconsistent with everything which has gone before that one cannot wonder Mrs Patrick Campbell, the first to play the part, remonstrated bitterly with Pinero, and is only surprised that he persisted in his original plan. Not only does Agnes determine to leave Lucas, but she is made to undergo a lightning change of heart, first throwing a bible on the fire then superstitiously rescuing it and setting off with the clergyman and his sister to live a life of prayer and remorse, castigating herself as a wicked woman, her relationship with Lucas as 'base and gross' and adjuring him to do all in his power to make up to his wife for the wrongs she has done her.

Again, as in *The Second Mrs Tanqueray*, this is not only incredible in itself, but thoroughly bad construction, since no preparation is made for these alarming new twists in Agnes's character. And as in *The Second Mrs Tanqueray* the blame for the errors of the last act cannot be laid at the door of the well-made play; though a case of some sort could be made out for the bible-burning scene as a *coup de théâtre*, however incredible it may be in relation to what has gone before (why should Agnes, child of a freethinker and herself always religiously heterodox, suddenly develop this 'instinctive' reverence for the book itself?), but the rest of the play fails on all levels as an adequate follow-up to the first three acts. It does not make sense in terms of character, as construction it comes as a disastrous anti-climax after the completely logical, brilliantly prepared climax of Agnes's submission to and disillusionment with Lucas, and above all it not only does not arise naturally, but does not even *seem* to arise naturally, from what has gone before. No wonder Mrs Campbell wrote of it later: 'The last act broke my heart.'

Perhaps in heed of criticisms that in this case he had not had the courage of his own convictions (as a dramatist, that is – as a man he no doubt heartily disapproved of Agnes and all she stood for) and had not gone far enough with his character, in his next drama, *Iris*, he went to the other extreme, and wrote the one play in which it may be said that he allows character to dominate the play at the expense of construction. Even Archer, though he persistently refers to its as 'one of the finest plays of our time', finds in it a number of faults of construction. Briefly, it concerns the chequered career of Iris Bellamy, an attractive young widow who will forfeit her fortune if she marries again. She feels drawn to a poor young idealist, while a wealthy financier, Maldonado, is passionately in love with her. To save herself from the foolishness of marrying the idealist she agrees to marry the financier, but he is infuriated when he finds out her true reasons. Reacting she takes the idealist as a lover but when he insists on going to Canada to make his fortune finds reasons for not going with him, even when she loses all her money and is soon living happily on Maldonado's money instead. She even sets up house with him and becomes his mistress. She is honestly mystified when the idealist, returned, cannot see the situation as 'sensibly' as she does, and even more surprised when Maldonado takes equal exception to her double-dealing and turns her out.

The character of Iris is one of satisfactory complexity: critics then and since have been divided on whether she should be seen as a shallow opportunist or a long-suffering and sorely put-upon woman. The trouble is that the play which contains her jumps a few vital steps. Archer, for all his enthusiasm, felt that Pinero had been culpably negligent in omitting to faire the *scène à faire*, in which Iris, having slipped almost accidentally into Maldonado's debt, slips that crucial step further, into being kept by him in a flat discreetly close to his own Mayfair home. Moreover, the play is ramblingly put together, in a way most unlike Pinero, with each act divided into a number of short scenes and a considerable lapse of time between beginning and end. The handling of the minor characters is quite perfunctory, and in general the play is a long way from well-madeness – as far away as Pinero ever got.

After that *His House in Order* shows him back on form: indeed, from every point of view it is one of his most satis-factory plays and a triumph of sheer craftsmanship in its ordering of its materials, so that the complicated story seems straight-forward and crystal-clear, and a succession of events which need not necessarily be inevitable is made to move with absolute certainty and naturalness from first to last. The whole action revolves round a believable but significant event, the inauguration of a memorial park given to the town by Filmer Jesson, a local landowner and M.P., in memory of his first wife, Annabel. Filmer has since married again, but his second wife, Nina, formerly his son's governess, does not live up to the standards created by his first: his private life is not kept in perfect order, as he would wish it, by her, and he has consequently brought in his first wife's sister to run his home. Nina is in disgrace, insulted and ignored by all, and already, like Hilary, Filmer's brother, we sympathize with her even before we meet her. However, hints are not lacking that she may get her own back: especially there is the suspiciously close relationship between Filmer's son Derek and a gloomy family friend called Maurewarde. And sure enough, Derek unearths in his mother's room, which has been assigned to him as a schoolroom to spite Nina, a collection of letters which prove that Maurewarde was Annabel's lover and the father of her child.

Before this, Nina, goaded beyond endurance, has refused point-blank to go to the opening ceremony at the park, knowing that what her priggish husband fears above all is scandal. Now she has in her hand the very weapon she needs to destroy those who have made her suffer most. Will she use it? In the central scene of the play Hilary, the only other person in the know, pleads, cajoles, and at last persuades her not to. She agrees after all to go to the ceremony. In the fourth act she gets her reward: Hilary disposes of Maurewarde, and then, after failing to make Filmer see reason any other way, tells him the truth. Filmer is forced at last to concede that Nina has qualities he had refused to see, and that she too has her rights: he will dismiss Annabel's accusing relatives, and at last give Nina a fair chance to keep his house in order her own way.

It may be asked how one can talk in terms of naturalness, credibility, inevitability even, about a plot which turns on such a hoary old melodramatic device as the discovery of a hidden letter which tells all. But this is just where Pinero's sheer technical brilliance works to best advantage. The device, if improbable, is certainly not impossible: such things have happened in life, and all the dramatist has to do is to convince us that this particular disclosure could and did happen here. The steps by which he achieves this have a logic which is irresistible. Annabel kept the letters – credible enough. She was killed quite unexpectedly in an accident, so that she had no chance to destroy them before her death. They are still concealed, therefore, in her room, which no one has been permitted to use since her death, though Nina thinks she ought to. Out of spite – as Nina, not unfairly sees it – Geraldine, Annabel's sister, proposes that Derek should be given the room as a schoolroom, thereby bypassing Nina's claims to it.

It has dramatic logic, therefore, that Geraldine's malice should bring about her own undoing. Equally, it adds the last touch of conviction that it should be the boy who finds the letters, though he does not know what they are: an adult would probably not find them unless he set out to look for them, but a child's curiosity and readiness to pursue an elusive mouse is just what would uncover them. So it all seems natural, if not inevitable. Only seems, perhaps, but then in drama what seems natural is natural – there are no legitimate and illegitimate illusions, only illusion achieved or not achieved.

In *His House in Order* Pinero achieves triumphantly all the illusions he sets out to achieve, and moreover creates a drama which, whether or not it says anything about Life, invents a group of thoroughly believable characters and says a lot about them as well as fitting them with unobtrusive art into a thoroughly satisfying dramatic pattern. If we suggest that in the area of straight drama *His House in Order* is from all points of view the best of all British attempts at the well-made play, and as telling now, for all we may since have found to say against the genre, as it was the day it was written, we shall not be too far off the mark.

After this, *Mid-Channel*, Pinero's only other straight drama and the last of his three plays which end with a suicide, need not long detain us. It is harsh enough in its picture of two self-centred partners in marriage going their own way after fourteen years of marital boredom, and the final irony whereby the wife, coming back somewhat deflated from her little adventure, is willing to pardon her husband for his but finds he will not return the compliment is neat enough. But again Zoe's suicide has no organic connection with anything we have learnt about her character before, and seems what it is, an arbitrary device to bring the play to an end. And the slangy talk of Pinero's demi-monde, particularly Peter, the *hausfreund* who points the moral, dates in a way that the conversation of his better educated characters never does. Already his writing is taking on again that unnatural hectoring tone when it comes to making his purpose plain which he had virtually lost since *The Profligate,* and the play in this respect looks forward rather to the clumsy satires like *The Big Drum* (1915) and *Child Man* (published 1930) in which he castigated his latterday *bêtes noires,* advertising and the image industries.

But in leaping ahead to consider all together the plays in which Pinero turned his well-made play technique to the requirements of drama – even, he may have hoped, of tragedy, though as far as I can find he never claimed so much – we have left aside a considerable number of more characteristic, and in some cases more successful plays: those occupying a territory somewhere between the basic farce of *Dandy Dick,* etc, and the serious, dramatic comedy of *His House in Order.* If we wanted to categorize these plays further we might say that *The Hobby Horse* (1886), *The Times* (1891) and *Letty* (1903) are satires, *Lady Bountiful* (1891), *The Princess and the Butterfly* (1897) and *The Thunderbolt* (1908) are lightweight sentimental dramas, *The Benefit of the Doubt* (1895) and *A Wife Without a Smile* (1904) are dramatic comedies, *The Gay Lord Quex* (1899) is a comedy of intrigue, *Preserving Mr Panmure* (1911) is a comedy light to the point of idiocy, and *Trelawny of the Wells* (1898), *The Mind-the-Paint Girl* (1912) and *The Freaks* (1918) are all comedies which in various ways depend on the contrast between theatre folk and ordinary mortals. But such categories are niggling and artificial: where Pinero excels at his best is in the adroit mixing of apparently incompatible elements – satire and sentiment, cynical realism and rosy nostalgia – into coherent, well-made plays which convince us, against all odds, that they are really all of a piece.

Thus all the 'satires' might equally well be classified as sentimental comedy. *The Times*, for example, which starts out as a satire on the pretensions of a *nouveau-riche* family, has running all through it a strain of real feeling in the romance of their unexpectedly sensible daughter with an unexpectedly sensible lord, and finally turns, gracefully and with no awkward grinding of gears, into a largely serious consideration by the parents of what they have lost in pursuit of the glittering social prizes which remain still, tantalizingly, just beyond their grasp.

The Hobby Horse, in which Shaw at the time noted 'character, humour, observation, genuine comedy, and literary workmanship' (he later took it all back) is more consistent, and still one of Pinero's most wholly attractive plays, which would no doubt stand up well to revival. One would call it sentimental comedy, except that it is not at all sentimental; comedy of sentiment then, about a wealthy woman who, heeding the appeals of social reformers to see the slums for herself (hence the mild satirical overtones) goes to live under an assumed name in the house of a poor curate. He falls in love with her (not knowing her true status), while her sailor step-son, whom she has never met, proves to be in love with the cleric's sister. The ensuing complications are neatly and wittily worked out, and the characterization is in Pinero's best unaffected manner. *Letty*, comparatively, is all over the place: its centrepiece, a rather funny scene in which an effete gentleman presides glumly over the farewell dinner of his married sister and her dismissed lover while at the next table the gentleman's girl-friend, who has decided that since he is married the best is to marry her employer, emphatically not a gentleman, is being entertained to a rowdy celebration supper. The setting-up of this situation is mildly satirical, the dénouement sentimental and silly.

Equally *Lady Bountiful, The Princess and the Butterfly* and *The Thunderbolt*, though primarily sentimental dramas, might just as well be labelled satires: the first starts in satirical comedy about society sponging, plunges into tearful drama in the middle, and ends in sheer melodrama; the second starts by being witty about the plight of two forty-year-olds who seek safety from making fools of themselves in a marriage of convenience but ends by growing dewily sentimental about their respective chancy romances with people little more than half their age. The third demolishes the pretensions of a high-class, genteel family by showing them involved in all sorts of undignified manœuvres over a disputed estate, but does so with more solemnity than satire.

The Gay Lord Quex, in which Pinero alarmingly seems to be reversing the point of The Profligate by letting his reformed rake get off scot-free and marry the young innocent with the blessings of all, has a brilliant third act of progressive revelations, which has been justly compared with the screen scene in The School for Scandal, but takes two whole acts working up to it in an 'elaborate series of trifling incidents' which, as Archer remarked, 'is at no point actually improbable; and yet we feel that a vast effort has been made to attain an end which, owing to the very length of the sequence of chances, at last assumes an air of improbability.' In other words, the means seems laborious, out of all proportion to the end.

There remain for consideration Preserving Mr Panmure, which isn't worth it, The Mind-the-Paint-Girl, which fits some plausible and amusing digs at the musical-comedy set and their hangers-on into an excessively casual and contrived plot about two rivals for the hand of a musical comedy queen, two oddities, A Wife Without a Smile and The Freaks, and two of Pinero's best plays, The Benefit of the Doubt and Trelawny of the Wells. The oddities are very odd. A Wife Without a Smile, called 'a comedy in disguise', caused a storm of protest at its appearance on account of what Hamilton Fyfe, one of Pinero's longest and loyalest admirers, called 'incidents so offensive' that even to recall them 'would repeat the offence' (and that in 1930!). Human nature being what it is, this inevitably arouses curiosity. But alas, it turns out that the daring consisted entirely of the jiggings of a dancing doll which indicated that Something Not Quite Nice was taking place on a sofa in the room above. It is hard to imagine that 1930 would have been quite so shocked about that as 1904 apparently was.

The Freaks, on the other hand, really is strange. It is a weird symbolic fantasy about a group of circus freaks, including a couple of midgets, a 'human knot' (female) and a 'skeleton dude', who are willed to a pretentious suburban family, create havoc when the son and daughter fall for the human knot and the skeleton dude respectively, and finally choose to go back to the sideshows, as a healthier and more normal environment. The idea is fetchingly odd, but though the play wrestles manfully with it, in the event Pinero's neat matter-of-fact technique is not at all up to dealing with more than a very few of its ironies and ambiguities. It was a mistake he did not get many more chances to make on the stage, though his faintly Barrie-esque fantasy *The Enchanted Cottage*, produced four years later, shows again how helpless he was, trained to be clear and precise in all things, when it came to dealing with a subject (husband and wife who are plain to everyone else but beautiful to each other in their enchanted cottage because they see with the eyes of love) which depends entirely on atmosphere, suggestion, and calculated vagueness.

In the other two plays, though, he is in various ways in his element. *The Benefit of the Doubt* is a play which works almost entirely on technique, and on technique, moreover, manipulated with a virtuosity and confidence which are almost brazen. In no first act, I think, does Pinero play with more outrageous ease and cunning on an audience's interests and expectations: the structure is one, shamelessly artificial, of delayed revelation. A case of some sort is going on, and the Emptages, family of one of those involved, await its outcome with breathless fascination. As messengers of all sorts arrive post-haste from court with fresh titbits we discover that it is a divorce case, no, a demand for legal separation, in which Theo, one of the daughters of the family, now Mrs Fraser of Locheen, figures in the ambiguous position of friend (or more?) of the husband.

To get to the bottom of the business it takes Mrs Emptage's sister, a worldly-wise bishop's wife, several minutes of cross-examination. From this it emerges that Theo has been acting,

at the very least, with conspicuous indiscretion in her dealings
with the offending husband and friend of the family Jack
Allingham – especially while her husband has been out of town.
At this point Theo arrives back, happily announcing that Mrs
Allingham's petition has been dismissed – though unfortunately the judge was a little rough on her, using words like
'careless' and 'indiscreet'. Left alone, Theo and her husband
have a scene; he says they must take refuge from the scandal
abroad; she says if he believes in her he will stand by her and
see it through. At length, finding him adamant, she slams out of
the house, leaving her wedding ring and a note. From this
latter the family conclude that she has gone to Jack Allingham,
and Mrs Cloys (the bishop's wife), Fraser, and a pompous
relation called Sir Fletcher Portwood set out in hot pursuit.
End of first act, audience helplessly eager to know what will
happen next.

The second act takes off at the same breakneck pace. The
family party make such good time they arrive at the Alling-
hams' first. They try embarrassedly to explain, but before they
can do so properly a note is sent up from Theo, asking Jack
to see her. He is about to refuse, but Mrs Allingham sees here
a heaven-sent opportunity to find out the truth: she can eaves-
drop on the conversation of Jack and Theo, and will thus soon
know whether there is anything shameful between them. This
works perfectly, and soon puts her mind at rest, but meanwhile
Jack has offered the overwrought Theo a glass of champagne.
Having eaten nothing all day and being now in a near-hysterical
state already, Theo rapidly succumbs to its influence, and proceeds to throw herself at Jack's head, begging him to run away
with her. It is time for Mrs Allingham to intervene, while
Theo's relations appear opportunely through the other door.
Theo does the only thing she can do: passes out.

How do you top that? One might fear that Pinero is about to
indulge in one of his last-act aberrations. Theo's suicide, maybe? Her religious conversion and retirement to a life of con-
templation and remorse? But no. Pinero is by now sufficiently
in command of his technique (and, be it said, his audience) to
opt for truth. No melodramatics, and no easy explanations. The

point Theo's behaviour in the second act makes is that she is already, unknown to herself, half in love with Jack or at least dangerously attracted to him. This is the truth behind the gossip and the slander, and it saves her just as, in different circumstances, a similar grain of truth destroys the heroines of *The Children's Hour*. She can face it, she can live with it, and in a while the world may resolve itself to live with her.

Mrs Cloys has the final word, and if not 'strong' or startling it is at least sensible and true. She will take Theo under her wing, she and her husband the bishop. Thus no one will think any more harm, and people will forget the harm they have thought – 'Oh, I don't think there will be many to wag evil tongues against Mrs Fraser a few months hence!' In effect, Pinero manages a *coup de théâtre* simply by so conspicuously avoiding one, choosing an anti-climax just where everyone expects a forced climax. The effective making of a well-made play could hardly go further.

If *The Benefit of the Doubt* is the play in which Pinero's technique is most dazzlingly, shamelessly on show, *Trelawny of the Wells* is the play in which he comes nearest, not only to banishing it from his audience's consciousness, but banishing it from his own as well. Ready for once, unpredictably, to give Pinero credit where credit was due, Shaw saw in it 'a certain delicacy which makes me loth to lay my fingers on it'. Of course he attributed this to the fact that in it Pinero was for once writing not about the present, which in Shaw's view he knew nothing about and had little sympathy with, but about the past, about the theatre as it was when he was five, in 1860, and about a world in which he was really, under it all, much more at home than in his own. There is no doubt some truth in this, at least insofar as it concerns Pinero's sympathy with and nostalgia for the period he was depicting. In it, one may suspect, Pinero comes as near as he does anywhere to wearing his heart on his sleeve, and a very gentle, old-world, sentimental heart it turns out to be.

The story is simple – for once really simple, and not just seemingly so. Rose Trelawny, popular star of Bagnigge Wells, is about to marry a young gentleman and abandon the stage for good. Her old companions in the theatre give her a farewell party, and she goes off to spend a sort of probationary period with her prospective husband's family. But she soon finds this boring, disgraces herself and leaves to return to the stage. The deep distress of all this has humanized her soul, however, and she is unable any more to play with conviction the silly old melodramas and sentimental tales in which she once shone. On the other hand, she is now woman enough to do justice to the simple, true dramas written by her friend Tom Wrench (a thinly disguised portrait of T. W. Robertson). And in the last act all is settled when not only is her erstwhile fiancé's grandfather prevailed upon to finance a production (spurred by sentimental recollections of her mother), but her fiancé, who has meanwhile renounced his family and taken to the stage, turns up as her leading man and the happy couple are reunited with the old man's blessing.

A slight story, though holding enough to keep the audience interested and constructed with all Pinero's ease and fluency. And strong enough to carry the super-structure which really interested him: the contrast between the old, worn-out drama which was the stock-in-trade of Bagnigge Wells and the, in its time, so new and realistic drama of Robertson, and the contrast between stage people and the stuffy rest of the world. Both contrasts are in some sense illusory. Robertson's drama, as we have seen, was not so different in essence from the sort of play it replaced; it merely changed the social and physical setting in which it took place, and as Allardyce Nicoll has aptly pointed out, if the line from *The Second Mrs Tanqueray* goes back directly to *Caste*, the line from *Caste* goes back just as directly and recognizably to *The Castle Spectre* and the wildest extremes of gothic melodrama. And the contrast between the warm, human stage folk and the cold, unnatural rest, if one of the hoariest clichés of theatre in life as in fiction, does not stand up to serious examination.

But the important thing is that Pinero believed them to be real; at least they were significant myths for him. So much so that he is able for once to accept all his characters in their own terms, to see the old actors like the Telfers, who were too old and too set in their ways to change, with sympathy of the same sort that he gives to the more obviously congenial Tom Wrench. He is even able to be kind to crusty old Sir William Gower, or anyway to appreciate from the inside what it must be like to see the world through Sir William's eyes.

We have said that this, ultimately, was what he failed to do with Paula Tanqueray or Agnes Ebbsmith; if he understood what it was like to be either, he recoiled from his understanding, and in recoiling wrecked the perfect mechanism of the well-made plays in which he had placed them. But in *Trelawny of the Wells* form and content are one, indivisible from beginning to end – it is the greatest triumph of Pinero's technique because the most lightly, unselfconsciously worn. It is no small thing to write a play as controlled and perfectly shaped as *His House in Order*, or as challengingly adroit as *The Benefit of the Doubt*. But it is a sign of greater art to write with such ease, real as well as apparent (*Dandy Dick* was written in under a month) farces which can hold the stage for eighty years and genuinely amuse after almost indefinite re-seeing. And perhaps it is best of all to write a play like *Trelawny of the Wells*, which is natural-seeming because it is natural, and well-made because its author could hardly any more do otherwise than make a play well, having forgotten more about sheer stagecraft than most of his more fashionable rivals would ever know.

Shaw and Wilde:
attack and a way of escape

Pinero's nostalgic tribute to Tom Robertson, founder of the movement in the British theatre of which he himself was culmination and the principal ornament, brings us to a convenient point to pause and consider what those who looked forward were looking forward to while Pinero looked lovingly back. For already, though Pinero's drama remained as popular as ever, it was losing or had lost its intellectual respectability. In 1893 *The Second Mrs Tanqueray* could, for all its compromises and sentimental short-cuts, create a genuine sensation, outrage the conservative and encourage the rebellious. It was, the American critic Clayton Hamilton said, 'the first play in the English language in which the dramatist dispensed with those aids to exposition – the soliloquy and the aside' – which, if it was not literally true, at least had enough truth in it to be significant. And it was morally as well as technically daring. By 1906, though, events had moved so fast in the theatre that Pinero was already regarded as a back number: *His House in Order* was received lukewarmly because in comparison with the constant excitements offered by the Barker-Vedrenne Company at the Royal Court it seemed old-fashioned and tame, even to those conservative critics who thirteen years earlier had found *The Second Mrs Tanqueray* altogether too much to swallow.

That this was so was due almost entirely to the enormous influence wielded by one man, George Bernard Shaw. Shaw did not believe in construction, he believed in ideas. Though his early idol Ibsen was a master of construction, as Archer never tired of demonstrating, Shaw chose to discount this side of his talents; it was as a bringer of ideas into the theatre that above all he revered Ibsen. He believed, therefore, that other things kept people in their seats in the theatre than the mere mechanical linking of scene to scene with clues and hints and secrets ripe for the telling and fateful meetings laboriously set up. To put things at their lowest – and Shaw was never one to shrink from doing that – theatre audiences had paid for their seats, or most of them had, and would therefore on the whole be inclined to remain in them in the faint hope, however groundless it might prove to be, of getting their money's worth. But there were other things. People would go to lectures on subjects that interested them, and sit them through without any of the theatre's artificial aids to concentration. They would engage in and listen to interesting conversation without any 'drama', any 'action', and come back for more. Were not these forms of appeal, or might they not be, sufficient in the theatre if only the cripple drama would gather enough confidence to throw away his crutches of 'technique' and walk?

Shaw might be right as far as his own plays were concerned, and in the proper, possibly the only way that his own talents might be expressed. But his teachings were quite likely to be fatal to anyone else. Of course a good play could not be put together by formula, and all worthwhile dramatists, however conscious of technique, have denied that it could – Pinero not least. But some guide lines, some sort of discipline, never comes amiss. And what Shaw was doing, and advocating, was disposing of the guide-lines, relying entirely on the inherent interest of what his plays were saying to carry him and them through. Naturally no one would deny that a successful impromptu speech, made at the right time, may have more effect than the most carefully constructed, scrupulously pre-planned script. But on the other hand no script is likely to be so bad as the fumbling, ill-timed impromptu speech, the desperate meanderings of a man who feels he should be saying something but has no clear or urgent idea of what. I am reminded of a phrase which has stayed with me from a long-forgotten novel. Someone is announced to be contemplating modelling as a career. 'But she can't,' cries a friend in desperation, 'She's just something that hangs down from her head!' Under Shaw's influence – and indeed among Shaw's own works – there have been too many plays which conscientiously, with almost religious fervour, eschewed all hint of well-made-play artifice, of forging connections where none necessarily were, and consequently ended up all too obviously as just something that hung down from their author's head.

But this is to anticipate. Long before Shaw was himself a dramatist, let alone a produced dramatist, he was a dramatic critic and theorist. And to find out just how his attack on the well-made play was mounted we must look back first of all to those days, and to the theory which he evolved from studying what was wrong with other dramatists' work years before he set about putting it right in his own.

From the outset Shaw made no secret of his own doctrinaire inclinations as a critic: announcing his enthusiastic adherence to the ideas of the 'Scandinavian realists', he added 'Never in my life have I penned an impartial criticism; and I hope I never may. As long as I have a want, I am necessarily partial to the fulfilment of that want, with a view to which I must strive with all my wit to infect everyone else with it.' When some of his dramatic criticism was first collected in 1900 he prefaced it with an 'Author's Apology' in which he makes the point still clearer.

> I must honestly warn the reader that what he is about to study is not a series of judgements aiming at impartiality, but a siege laid to the theatre of the XIXth Century by an author who had to cut his own way into it at the point of the pen, and throw some of its defenders into the moat.
>
> Pray do not conclude from this that the things hereinafter written were not true, or the deepest and best things I knew how to say. Only, they must be construed in the light of the fact that all through I was accusing my opponents of failure because they were not doing what I wanted, whereas they were often succeeding very brilliantly in doing what they themselves wanted.

And what, precisely, did they want which Shaw thought so objectionable? Above all, they wanted a combination of two things: a neat, well-made construction à la Sardou and the appearance of verisimilitude in handling domestic relations à la Robertson. As we have seen, there is no inherent reason why these two ideals should go hand in hand, but they reach hailing distance at least in the works of Robertson himself, shake hands in the adaptations of Sydney Grundy, and are inseparables by the time we get to Henry Arthur Jones and Pinero.

Shaw was inclined, on principle, to object to either. As he wrote of Jones in a kindly mood, 'In the born writer the style is the man; and with the born dramatist, the play is the subject.' So he objected to anything which interfered with the free development of the subject, as the canons of what he christened Sardoodledum obviously did. He also objected to the idea of surface verisimilitude – the creation of an impression of truth to life by the pointless proliferation of irrelevant detail which always tended to distract eye, ear and mind from the broader significance of the action. But more than to either of these standards individually he objected to them both together, combined into that curious hybrid the well-made English drawing-room drama. For this was nothing more to him than a confidence trick: first human life was falsified by being cut arbitrarily to fit the moulds of Sardoodledum, then the first deception was pasted over with a more or less plausible imitation of the real thing, so that audiences would not notice how their reactions were being manipulated.

This might not matter too much if the end product was a Pinero farce, which did not pretend to make any statement about society or human life, but it did matter very much if this imposter were to start claiming serious intentions. Shaw objected so much to Pinero's dramas not so much because of their differences from Ibsen as because of the similarities: superficially, Pinero and Ibsen might seem to be writing the same sort of play, but whereas Ibsen's aim was to re-examine the conventions and where necessary undermine them, Pinero's was insidiously to bolster them up while only appearing to put them daringly in question. Whether Pinero intended anything of the sort may of course be questioned. He simply set about using materials from the social life around him to produce gripping stories, and accepted the conventions which were generally held to govern behaviour in polite society at their face value. They were the *données* of any given dramatic situation, and that was all there was to it. Not that this excused him in Shaw's eyes: after all, even a deviously cunning apologist for conventional morality would be preferable to someone who did not even see that there was a question to be asked.

In any case, there was a further point to be considered. The aesthetic conventions of the well-made play depended on the moral conventions of the society it was written about and for. All the drama arose from the conflicts which occurred when these social conventions were transgressed and the transgressor had in some way to be brought to book. If the dramatist accepted for a moment that the conventions were at best a polite fiction, at worst a monstrous imposition stifling all true social progress, and in either case that they were not as immutable as one of nature's laws, then he was cutting the ground from under his own feet. Ibsen had done this willingly, eagerly. But in doing so he had gradually confined himself more and more to dealing with extraordinary characters, because the ordinary were ordinary mainly because they continued, by and large, to pay lip-service to the very conventions he was out to destroy. And ordinariness, drama based on the behaviour of ordinary people in only slightly extraordinary situations, was one of the things the popular British dramatists of the 1890s held most dear.

And yet, worst of all crimes, they were not invincibly ignorant; they were not doing as they did just because they were unaware of Ibsen and therefore knew no better. As I suggested in the last chapter, the most important single factor in accounting for the difference between *The Profligate* and *The Second Mrs Tanqueray* in Pinero's work is undoubtedly the advent of Ibsen. And Henry Arthur Jones, though he might strenuously deny any possibility that Ibsen had influenced him, did not hesitate to adapt and water down Ibsen in his own early days as a dramatist. Shaw, of course, took the point. Drawing a sharp contrast between the most successful dramas of the 1880s and those of the 1840s he says:

The change is evident at once. In short, a modern manager need not produce The Wild Duck, but he must be very careful not to produce a play which will seem insipid and old-fashioned to playgoers who have seen The Wild Duck, even though they may have hissed it.

How, then, was this phony, hollow drama Shaw found all around him, and, more annoying still, profiting vastly from its disreputable success, to be shot down? The obvious answer might seem to be: by comparing it unfavourably with the possibilities of a new, liberated drama such as Shaw had in mind, boldly careless of form and disdainful of the mere accidents of cup-and-saucer surface realism. But Shaw was too shrewd a tactician for that. He knew perfectly well that this, in prospect, would alarm the conservative playgoer so much that he would cleave all the more closely to what he knew and felt safe with. No: what was necessary first of all was to discredit the well-made drawing-room drama, make it such a laughing-stock that it would be swept from the stage. Once that stage was empty, after all, anything might happen. . . .

And so Shaw set systematically discrediting the well-made play not by opposing it with the standards to which he himself owed allegiance, but with the very standards its proponents asked for it to be judged by. Constructed, was it? Well, Shaw would just show his readers how jerry-built most of these construction jobs were, how haphazardly the various parts were propped together. Realistic, was it? Well, Shaw would expose every sham, every half-truth, every device employed to make what was inherently incredible seem credible, what was demonstrably false look like the truth.

And that is what he did. We have seen his method in action in *The Second Mrs Tanqueray*, and very effective it is as far as it goes. But it does not bear much analysis. For after all, what Shaw objects to is not stage convention in itself, but stage convention which tries to disguise itself as something else. Most of his own plays use conventions just as extravagant as Tanqueray's retirement to write letters, or the multiplicity of doors and postman's visits, but he does not try to present them as anything but what they are, and it is above all the puritan in him that is outraged by the apparent ease with which Pinero puts one over on his audience. Nor does Shaw himself object to stock characters – many of his own are more blatantly from stock than anything in the drama he is condemning. But blatantly – that is the point. He can take stereotypes for what they are – he loves the best of the melodrama surviving into the 1890s, and constantly uses it as a stick with which to beat more effete forms – but he resents intensely a stereotype tricked out with borrowed graces as an original creation.

And so on. It is easy to refute Shaw in principle on almost every objection he raises to the well-made play – though of course in his practical criticism of particular points in particular plays he is often devastatingly right. Where Shaw is not so easy to controvert is in his views on the social, moral and intellectual mission of the drama, for that is a question of faith, and there it is every man for himself. Be that as it may, there is no arguing the success that Shaw's criticism had at the time. Not that alone – also slowly influential was the appearance in London during the 1890s of plays by Ibsen, certainly, but also by Maeterlinck, Brieux, Strindberg, Hauptmann, Sudermann and others. Many of these were given their first important showing in London by J. T. Grein and his Independent Theatre – which also, incidentally, happened to produce Shaw's own first play, *Widowers' Houses*, in 1892.

But undoubtedly it was Shaw above all who destroyed public confidence in the well-made play, succeeding all too well in his declared aim of surrounding his opponents 'with a subtle atmosphere of absurdity'. In 1884 *Saints and Sinners* was outrageously daring; in 1893 *The Second Mrs Tanqueray* caused an uproar. By 1900 Henry Arthur Jones was enjoying his last real triumph as a dramatist of the moment and by 1905 Pinero had one of his best plays judged old-fashioned. There was, as far as exciting new British drama was concerned, a vacuum in the theatre, a vacuum created by Shaw. And who was ready to rush in and fill it, to become the most successful and talked about dramatist of the 1900s? Why George Bernard Shaw, of course.

It would, of course, be perfectly possible – it has been done many times – to show how Shaw, the great eclectic, did not scruple to use even the conventions of the despised well-made play to his own ends when it suited him to do so. He could parody the familiar drawing-room problem play in *Mrs Warren's Profession*, relying on the fact that the presence of a 'Mrs' in a play's title, from Pinero's just-produced *Second Mrs Tanqueray* right up to *The Last of Mrs Cheyney*, could always be relied upon to excite the right sort of wrong sort of expectations about the presence in the cast of a woman with a secret. He could use the conventions of popular farce for his own purposes in *You Never Can Tell* – and find the trick turned against him, since irritatingly enough many in the audience failed to notice the vital Shavian differences. But to pursue this line would help little, for Shaw's work as a dramatist is in fundamental rebellion against the well-made play, and what we are interested in is how, despite him, it managed to continue. And here the main exception he allowed to his general views on English drama of 1890s becomes relevant.

For even at his most doctrinaire Shaw was not entirely hostile to the native British drama of his own day. He occasionally said nice things even about Pinero and Henry Arthur Jones; perhaps from perversity he praised *Guy Domville* (1895), the major (and final) assault of the novelist Henry James on the citadel of drama, which tried to pour the matter of a Jamesian novel into the form of the well-made drawing-room drama, with odd and scarcely dramatic results. But in all his strictures against the well-made play and its falsities, there is only one figure who consistently retains Shaw's regard: Oscar Wilde. And if Shaw, by the sharpness of his tongue and the prestige of his example, aided by changing conventions of public and private morality as the new century wore on, managed to drag the more serious elements in British drama away from the well-made, realistic drawing-room drama, he still left the particular area which Wilde ruled over in his heyday safe from any too damaging attack. Give Shaw the serious theatre, and he would let drawing-room comedy alone to fend for itself.

Thus it was that Wilde, apparently peripheral to the drama

of his time, should become after his disgrace, enforced retirement from the theatre and death a crucial example for the
younger generation. Wilde's cardinal virtue as a dramatist
was he was primarily a comedian. Though in his aesthetic days
he dabbled in overblown verse drama with *Vera; or the Nihilists*
(1880) and *The Duchess of Padua* (1883), and returned to such
essentially closet plays with *Salome* (1892, written in French)
and *A Florentine Tragedy*, an ironic one-act verse drama written
in 1895, his success in the theatre was won entirely with plays
which mirrored the ordinary theatrical tastes of his day: *Lady
Windermere's Fan* (1892), *A Woman of No Importance* (1893),
An Ideal Husband (1895) and *The Importance of Being Earnest*
(1895).

The first three of these give at first glance every appearance
of being conventional drawing-room dramas. The beautiful
young Lady Windermere proves, unbeknown to her, to be the
daughter of Mrs Erlynne, a woman with a past. And Mrs
Erlynne, returning after years in which she deserted husband
and child, disastrously as it turned out, to run off with a lover,
finds her own daughter about to make the same mistake. In a
belated access of mother-love she sacrifices herself to ensure
her daughter's happiness. In *A Woman of No Importance* the
woman with a past is Mrs Arbuthnot, mother of Gerald, a young
man who has been kept, like Lady Windermere, in ignorance
of his own parentage. The problem this time arises when he
is offered a job as Lord Illingworth's secretary – something
which could lead on to great things and allow him to marry
the girl he loves. But Lord Illingworth is, without knowing it,
Gerald's father; Mrs Arbuthnot fears the consequences of the
appointment, and is forced to admit why when Gerald is about
to strike Lord Illingworth for insulting his fiancée, with the
third act curtain-line 'Stop, Gerald, stop! He is your own
father!' The 'ideal husband' is Sir Robert Chiltern, an ambitious
and high-principled politician whose dark secret is that he once,
in younger days, sold a state secret to a foreign power. Another
woman with a past, Mrs Cheveley, turns up to blackmail him,
but is thwarted by Lord Goring, a friend of the Chilterns who
happens to have evidence that she is a thief and can engineer a

piece of counter-blackmail. In retaliation Mrs Cheveley tries to wreck the Chilterns' marriage over a supposed liaison between Lady Chiltern and Lord Goring, but the plot backfires and only brings the Chilterns closer together.

Not only are these, apparently, ordinary society dramas, but they are society dramas of a decidedly old-fashioned kind, littered with asides and soliloquies. What then saves them, for Shaw and for us? Primarily, I think, their entire shamelessness. Wilde does not give the impression, even for a moment, that he takes all this nonsense seriously. The plots are creaking old contrivances, and far from trying to disguise the fact he glories in it. They are strong enough to hold up a glittering display of epigrams, delivered for the most part by characters – the Duchess of Berwick, Lady Hunstanton, even Lord Goring – who are irrelevant to most of the main action except as a sort of mocking chorus, and that is all that the plot is there for. Wilde's element of barefaced charlatanism appealed to Shaw: at least if he appeared to be upholding conventional morality, he was doing it with so little conviction, and with tongue so evidently in cheek, that no one could take it seriously, and therefore no one could take it amiss.

The message of Wilde's drama became even plainer in *The Importance of Being Earnest*, where at last even the slightest pretence of seriousness is dropped and joy reigns unconfined in a farcical farrago about two suitors, two girls under the erroneous impression they are engaged to a man called Earnest, a gorgon-like mother-in-law to be, an absent-minded nurse and a complicated history of a baby inadvertently left in a handbag at Victoria Station left-luggage office, the Brighton line. Of course, by the same token this might be the most serious of all Wilde's plays, but that is another matter. The point is that here all the machinery of the well-made play finds a triumphantly and unarguably proper use. The convention is paramount: nobody really talks or acts like this, or certainly not for more than a few moments at a time, but, to paraphrase Turner's remark to a lady who objected that she never saw sunsets as he painted them, don't we all wish they did?

Wilde disappeared prematurely from the theatre, but the

model remained. Pinero and Henry Arthur Jones might be discredited, and with them the sort of drama they represented. But if that sort of craftsmanship was considered obsolete in the straight play, it was still entirely acceptable in light comedy; if drama had broken out of the drawing-room, comedy still found its natural home there. And in no writer did it preside there more confidently and compellingly than in W. Somerset Maugham.

W. Somerset Maugham

With Pinero, as we have seen, the well-made play in Britain reached its high point in critical repute and then passed it, so that by the time his last considerable play, *His House in Order*, was produced in 1906, its very well-madeness, while generally agreed, was the thing most damagingly held against it: Shaw had shown us better, the Barker-Vedrenne company had driven home the lesson by presenting an illuminating cross-section of the best world theatre had to offer, and Pinero's tragedy was that he remained the prisoner of a convention which, even at its best, prevented those who adopted it from rising ever above the second-rate.

So, one might reasonably imagine, the well-made play was a thing of the past, something which might perhaps appeal to the less demanding theatre audience for a while, but which could certainly not give rise to lasting drama in the enlightened twentieth century. In London, at any rate, the age of Pinero was over and the age of Shaw just begun: from being our most influential dramatic critic he had leapt spectacularly during the last decade to being our most influential dramatist. But things are seldom quite so simple and clearcut. And who should be the next major dramatist to emerge on the London scene after Shaw but a man who exemplified in his work all the concern for craftsmanship and construction, in a word for well-madeness, which Shaw despised and had apparently taught the rest of the thinking world to despise too? William Somerset Maugham, who in 1908, after some years as a mildly successful novelist and quite unsuccessful dramatist, took the London theatre by storm with no fewer than four plays running simultaneously.

How to explain this curious turn of events? Principally by

one fact, and one fact alone. Maugham hit below the belt: he wrote comedies. True, Shaw wrote comedies too, and everything he said about ideas in drama, intelligence in drama applied quite as much to comedy as to drama – more, in effect, since he appreciated better than anyone that the best way to sugar the pill of ideas for an unwilling and suspicious British audience was to present them as amusingly as possible. But critics and everybody else persisted in applying different standards to comedy and to drama. Ibsen (not to mention Ibsen as interpreted by Shaw – a quite distinct phenomenon) might provide the model for high seriousness in the theatre, but when it came to comedy there were still enough left who thought it a sufficient aim for the dramatist just to keep people amused. And on the whole, the more neatly and 'theatrically' he did it, the better they would be pleased. This Maugham, superlatively, did; and by his practice managed to win back a certain area – very roughly what we would call comedy of manners – for the despised and rejected well-made play. If a dramatist tried, as Maugham himself later did, to write a serious drama in the same artificially tidy form he was likely to be accused sternly of superficiality. But if he wrote comedies this way, so what? Was it not after all the business of comedy to be superficial? And if they turned out finally to be less superficial than they seemed, well, that might be a pleasant, unexpected bonus but did not in any way effect the initial judgement.

It is symptomatic of the mental climate in which Maugham achieved his first successes that J. T. Grein, founder of the Independent Theatre and first English producer of *Ghosts*, should have written in the *Sunday Times* like this about *Lady Frederick*:

> It is not quite a lifelike comedy, nor is it free from the artifice and calculation which was customary in the days of the 'well-made play'. There is something mechanical in the humour and in the characters which would have prompted me if I had read the manuscript to change the time of the action. To me these delightful, well-spoken, gracefully conversational people are not of today. I see them in

the formal surroundings and clothes of the late sixties; I see them even more forcibly in the picturesque raiment of powder and wig. Indeed, if light verse were substituted for prose, Mr Maugham would have found in his story exquisite material for a poetic comedy. But I take the work as it is presented, and undoubtedly, despite its corsetted form and somewhat antiquated devices, it has drawn . . .

Clearly, Grein is here both sounding a warning note about any hint of the discredited 'days of the "well-made play"' (as though they were generations ago, instead of a mere ten years or so), and providing a variety of get-outs. If the play were in period it would be all right. (Why? because life was less real in the 1860s than the 1900s?). If it were in verse it would be entirely acceptable (presumably because verse inures us to artifice, but prose is, or ought to be, real and earnest). But even as it is, it has charm, and it is after all a comedy, so we cannot judge it too seriously. And if Grein the Ibsenite thought so (Shaw the Ibsenite having been happily translated to a higher sphere than drama criticism), then a lot of less exacting people were going to think so too.

So Maugham the cynical comedian was granted at least a conditional, limited sort of intellectual respectability. These might be a slight measure of disagreement over whether he was writing trivial plays for serious people or serious plays for trivial people – he himself would no doubt have said he was doing both, depending on which way audiences chose to take him – but there was no doubt that triviality entered into it somewhere, and that, oddly enough, provided a convenient critical loophole for almost everyone. But success, as we have said, did not come to him overnight. His first surviving play, a one-acter called *Marriages are Made in Heaven*, was written as early as 1897 and received its solitary production (by Reinhardt of all people) in 1902 as part of a dramatic cabaret in a Berlin café-theatre. A full-length drama, *A Man of Honour*, was written in 1898 and first publicly performed in 1904, with little success. Two more, *The Explorer* and *Loaves and Fishes*, went hopelessly on their rounds of agents and managements before Maugham's fame of 1908 got them produced. And even *Lady Frederick* had to wait five years for production, while the other two which made his name in 1908, *Mrs Dot* and *Jack Straw*, had to wait respectively four and three years.

Perhaps it was as well, for by 1908 the theatre was clearly ready for a reaction against the reaction against the well-made play. Provided, of course, that nobody recognized it as such. Shavian principles made such an appeal to the incurably puritanical, incurably romantic English that the well-made play, like 'mere entertainment', has hardly had a decent word said for it since. But Shaw recognized in one way, and Maugham proved in another, that mere entertainment, however sternly pushed out at the door, will somehow contrive to creep back in a different guise through the window. Shaw managed to make entertainment respectable by teaching it ideas, but only at the risk of having the ideas dismissed as not really serious because they were found in such light company. Maugham took the safer course of opting from the outset for intellectual disreputability, and in consequence survived for twenty-two years of theatrical success as the delight of those who did not care for ideas and the *péché mignon* of those who did.

The tally of Maugham's full-length produced plays is twenty-six, not counting three translations; of these eighteen are readily accessible in the six volumes of his *Collected Plays*, and one of those excluded, *The Letter*, is nevertheless well known. Obviously it would be tedious and pointless to go through these one by one considering how far and in what way they are well-made, where and if they fail, and how far in such cases it is craftsmanship or lack of craftsmanship which is at fault. But if we select characteristic examples of Maugham's comedy and his drama, and pay particular attention to what he, coolest and most perceptive of auto-critics, has said about them, some sort of pattern may begin to emerge. That there is a pattern of sorts is suggested by the very disposition of the *Collected Plays*. Each volume contains three (perhaps the main reason that *The Letter* is excluded is that threes into nineteen won't go without spoiling the symmetry). They are arranged almost but not quite in chronological order. Volume One is all light comedies: *Lady Frederick, Mrs Dot, Jack Straw.* Volume Two and Volume Three contain comedies of slightly more weight: respectively *Penelope, Smith* and *The Land of Promise* and *Our Betters, The Unattainable (Caroline)* and *Home and Beauty.* That gets us up to 1919, leaving aside for a later volume only one drama, *Caesar's Wife* (1918). Volume Four gathers together the three later comedies, *The Circle* (1919), *The Constant Wife* (1926) and *The Breadwinner* (1930), which have in common principally a rather more clearly perceptible moral intent, even though their morals are paradoxical, than those which have gone before. Volume Five is all 'strong' drama: *Caesar's Wife, East of Suez* (1922) and *The Sacred Flame* (1928); presumably *The Letter* (1926) would also come here if neatness allowed. And Volume Six gathers together Maugham's three comic-dramatic unclassifiables, *The Unknown* (1920), *For Services Rendered* (1932) and *Sheppey* (1933).

I suppose by general consent it would be agreed that the last three are about the least achieved of all the plays Maugham elected to preserve. Just above these in critical estimation would come the strong dramas, or melodramas as the less charitable would say – less charitable not because melodrama is necessarily to be regarded as in itself a bad thing, but because it seems that in these plays melodrama is not what Maugham set out to produce. The least dated of them, by far, is the quietest and earliest, *Caesar's Wife.* Then would come the comedies, order very much according to individual taste but with *The Land of Promise* no doubt in the lowest place. So, if we may judge at all by the concensus of critical opinion, a sort of pattern does emerge. And it would seem to be this: as Maugham progressed in the theatre, he became readier to write 'serious', i.e. non-comic plays, and as he did so he achieved considerably less, or at least less lasting, success. How far this was the result of limitations in the convention he chose to work in, how far of his attempts to depart from that convention, and how far of purely personal limitations which had little at all directly to do with his approach to dramatic form, a closer look at the plays themselves may help us to decide.

The best place to start, no doubt, is at the beginning, with the three plays that made Maugham's name. Each of them is quite unmistakably a well-made play; none can be called by any stretch of the imagination a play of ideas, for even the hints of social satire in them are so slight as to be negligible, the slightest dusting of gilt on the gingerbread. *Lady Frederick*, which is probably the best of the three, will stand fairly enough for them all. In Act One we are introduced to Lady Frederick Berolles, loved to distraction by a much younger man, Charles Mereston; Lady Frederick's brother Gerald O'Mara, who loves to distraction Admiral Carlisle's daughter Rose; Paradine Fouldes, who has been commissioned by Charles Mereston's mother (Paradine's sister) to put a stop to her son's liaison with Lady Frederick; and Captain Montgomerie, a gentleman of shady background eager for his own reasons to marry Lady Frederick.

The play consists simply – if anything so casually accomplished can be called simple – of the arrangement and rearrangement of the pieces in this puzzle until they fit together neatly, just in time for the final curtain. Act One gets Gerald O'Mara engaged to Rose Carlisle, tells us that Lady Frederick is in debt, discloses that Paradine Fouldes was formerly in love with Lady Frederick, sees Lady Frederick and Paradine reach an impasse when he threatens to tell Charles about her crowded love-life and she counters with some compromising letters she holds about Charles's father's peccadillos, establishes Lady Frederick's good nature by making her offer the letters to Paradine for him to destroy (he refuses) and then at the curtain reveals that Captain Montgomerie has a financial hold over Gerald O'Mara and is willing to use it to get what he wants.

In the second act the plot thickens. Gerald and Lady Frederick discuss their financial troubles, but Lady Frederick refuses Paradine's offer of £7,000 for the Mereston letters. Captain Montgomerie returns to the attack: he now holds all Gerald's bills, and will return them only if Lady Frederick accepts him. To separate her son from Lady Frederick, Lady Mereston tries some blackmail of her own, using a letter in which Lady Frederick avows a former affair. Lady Frederick explains this to the satisfaction of Paradine and Charles, then burns the Mereston letters, without disclosing what they contain, and dismisses Charles. Distraught, he apologizes for his mother and begs Lady Frederick to marry him. She says she will answer the following day.

Act Three unravels the by now pretty tangled threads of the plot in a textbook dénouement. First, to disillusion Charles, Lady Frederick lets him see her as she really is without makeup and other artificial aids (this scene, thought daring at the time, was the original great talking-point of the play). He dutifully repeats his proposal, but is evidently relieved when Lady Frederick refuses. Next Gerald arrives with his prospective father-in-law, the Admiral: he has confessed all and the Admiral has settled his debts with Captain Montgomerie. The Admiral then proposes to Lady Frederick, who refuses him also. Next Montgomerie arrives and proposes again; though he no longer has a hold over Gerald, he still has Lady Frederick's bills with which to blackmail her. But Paradine, who has also called this crowded morning, pays him off and dismisses him; left alone, Paradine at once proposes to Lady Frederick, who accepts him.

Not, it will be seen, a plot exactly lacking in contrivance. Indeed, the contrivance is deliberately insisted on: if it is unlikely, for instance, that Lady Frederick should have so conveniently acquired compromising letters addressed to Lord Mereston, it is doubly unlikely that at the same time Lady Mereston should have acquired a compromising letter from Lady Frederick. But in the light comedy convention of the well-made play the two coincidences as it were cancel out; their duplication and obtrusively neat matching somehow disarms criticism by making it clear that they are no more than a device. Either we accept and enjoy such shameless toying with artifice for its own sake, or we reject it out of hand, but there are no half measures possible. And if we do accept it, at least the way Maugham presents it makes us accept it open-eyed; we cannot feel, as opponents of the well-made drama resentfully felt, that something is being put over on us, we are being cheated into accepting as true some comment on life when its truth has been demonstrated largely on rigged evidence. That this is an over-simplified and insufficient ground for judging dramatic effect goes without saying, but in the 1900s in Britain the delayed effect of Shaw's strictures on the drama of the previous generation had been to establish such a limitedly naturalistic view of things as the most intellectually respectable form of critical orthodoxy – ironically, since whatever he was against in others, elementary naturalism was the last thing Shaw wanted or intended to practise himself.

So for Maugham's first audiences, as for later ones, it was the very improbability of, say, the succession of proposals received by the irresistible Lady Frederick in the course of one morning, or the way that Jack Straw, a waiter posing as an archduke, turns out in the end to be an archduke after all, which helped to recommend the plays; the author made no bones about it, and you knew where you were with him, just as you knew where you were with Wilde when he subtitled *The Importance of Being Earnest* 'an improbable comedy'. Wilde had finally, after toying with the well-made drama in three plays, summoned up the courage to write the first British masterpiece of artificial comedy for nearly 200 years; Maugham followed in his footsteps, and at once became the licensed jester-in-chief of the London stage. He was, it was said, cynical; he was certainly 'not serious'. But since he would be the first to agree with this judgement, what more was there to say?

The reputation of cynical joker was to prove, as it turned out, an invaluable cover. It saw Maugham happily through many featherweight trifles like *Penelope, Caroline* and *Home and Beauty.* Even when he ventured a little away from precision-tooled artificial comedy with *The Land of Promise*, a rather ramshackle rehandling of the *Taming of the Shrew* theme in a rural Canadian setting, it got him by. And as for his few attempts at drama, like *The Tenth Man* (1909) and *Landed Gentry* (also called *Grace*, 1910), which dealt respectively with unscrupulous dealings in the city and heartlessness in the squirearchy, well, they served their turn, neither succeeding nor failing spectacularly, and their author soon showed himself as ready to forget them as everyone else was. But the real advantage of Maugham's dramatic persona became evident when, with *Our Betters* (written in 1915), he began to modify his devotion to artificial comedy in the full, near-farcical sense of the term. What he was up to in most of the plays he wrote between *Our Betters* and *The Constant Wife* (1926) is best described in his own words (even though he confuses the issue by using 'artificial comedy' in a rather special sense):

> These plays . . . are written in the tradition which flourished so brightly in the Restoration period, which was carried on by Goldsmith and Sheridan, and which, since it has had so long a vogue, may be supposed to have something in it that peculiarly appeals to the English temper. The people who do not like it describe it as artificial comedy, and by the epithet foolishly think they condemn it. It is drama not of action, but of conversation. It treats with indulgent cynicism the humours, follies and vices of the world of fashion. It is urbane, sentimental at times, for that is in the English character, and a trifle unreal. It does not preach; sometimes it draws a moral, but with a shrug of the shoulders as if to invite you to lay no too great stress on it . . . The first person the author of comedy must consider from the standpoint of comedy is himself.

Most of Maugham's earlier plays could not be accused of pointing any moral, no matter how lightly and casually. This was a major ingredient of their success. When, with *Our Betters*, he began to figure as a *censor morum*, according at least to his own rather eccentric lights, he reaped the reward of cultivated frivolity: no one consciously noticed. Thus without forfeiting his privileged jester status, and without having to modify at all the well-made play convention in which he was accustomed to work, he was able to deepen his plays and make entirely serious points about society, and indeed about Life, without at once being told by critics that this was impermissible within the artificially ordered form he had chosen.

Before we go on to see exactly how Maugham managed to

do this, however, we may as well look briefly at the avowedly, or anyhow allegedly, serious plays he was writing in these years. Up to and including *The Sacred Flame* (1928) there are five: the others are *Caesar's Wife*, *The Unknown*, *East of Suez* and *The Letter*. All of them have obviously serious themes: respectively marital fidelity and self-sacrifice; religious differences as an impediment to marriage; miscegenation; miscegenation again with marital fidelity thrown in; and in *The Sacred Flame* euthanasia. All of them rigidly eschew comedy in their handling of these themes. They were accepted with varying degrees of seriousness at the time; now few if any would be taken very seriously at all.

It is easy to see why. *The Letter* and *The Sacred Flame* are both in effect detective plays. In the first the curtain goes up on a shooting, and the rest of the play is cunningly built on the progressive revelation of the true circumstances in which Leslie Crosbie killed Geoffrey Hammond. In the second Maurice Tabret, long paralysed as a result of an air crash, dies mysteriously at the end of the first act, and suspicion points to his wife, who is pregnant by his brother, but in the end his mother admits that she brought about his happy release. In both the drama is built, quite efficiently, from the posing of a mystery and its methodical unravelling. Obviously this is a 'well-made' method of putting a play together; equally obviously, by keeping the audience in the dark about the facts of the case for so long Maugham precludes himself from any very searching consideration of the problems on which the plays appear to be based – they end up not as problem plays, but as plays which play with problems. Which is of course a perfectly legitimate way of going about things, but not, after all, a very 'serious' way. On the other hand, we would be hasty to conclude that the plays are prevented from dealing with serious problems seriously just because they are well-made. After all, all whodunits should be well-made, but that does not necessarily mean that all well-made plays need stick at being whodunits.

East of Suez does not deserve even so much consideration: it is probably the silliest play Maugham wrote, and he probably knew it. It was written as a spectacle, for elaborate production by Basil Dean, and the melodramatic tale of East and West failing markedly to meet in the marriage of a very correct Englishman and a very unscrupulous half-Chinese with a past no doubt served this purpose well enough. There is little more to be said of it, except that Maugham later remarked on it as virtually the only time he composed a detailed scenario before actually writing a play. He thought this simplified the writing considerably, but tended to make the result lifeless and mechanical; in this case it is difficult not to agree with him.

Caesar's Wife and *The Unknown* are in quite a different class; *Caesar's Wife* is arguably the best non-comic play Maugham wrote, and *The Unknown* almost certainly the worst – at any rate it is certainly by far the least accomplished of all those he chose to preserve in the collected edition. No doubt what Maugham tells us about the genesis of the two plays is relevant here. *Caesar's Wife* he records, arose from a reading of *La Princesse de Clèves* and an urge to transfer its pattern – a virtuous wife hopelessly in love with another man but determined to do nothing about it, a loving husband who knows and wisely understands, the other man who also acts honourably throughout – to a modern setting. *The Unknown*, on the other hand, came from a desire to write a play about two people kept apart by religious differences beyond the control of either. In other words, *Caesar's Wife* started from a pattern, *The Unknown* started from people. And it shows.

In *Caesar's Wife* Maugham was faced with what he always responded to best, a technical challenge. Given a pattern of behaviour from Madame de Lafayette, he saw it first and foremost as a challenge to write a play in which everyone involved behaves entirely well and honourably; moreover, he wanted to do this, as a practical dramatist and also perhaps as a discreet moralist, in such a way that they should all be believable and that none should be insipid, as the virtuous usually are on stage. He modified the essentials of the original plot line only very slightly, to make the husband significantly older than the wife and wiser and more dignified in his understanding of the situation, and to make the young man loved by the wife a more interesting and estimable character; he also removed the most evident contrivance of the book, the husband's over-convenient death. In part, as he admitted in his introduction to the relevant volume of the *Collected Plays*, he was the more willing to write a play in which all the characters were estimable in that 'I had been often reproached for writing only about unpleasant people, . . . though I did not think the reproach justified' – yet another aspect of the technical challenge, this time delivered from outside the author's own unassisted impulses.

The result of Maugham's efforts is a play of classical direct-ness and simplicity, well-made less by virtue of an elaborate contrivance of cause and effect than by the deliberate stripping away of inessentials, so that the logical progression of the action is left clear and uncluttered for all to see. In a sense it is dated, since the code of honour by which the characters attempt to live and in general succeed in living is of its time but not of ours, and the appeal to patriotism by which the heroine is persuaded to face her dilemma and live with it as best she may instead of arranging a fairly easy escape also has a very period ring to it. But despite moments of sentimentality the play has no essential falseness; it has a certain truth to its own time which gives it a lasting truth, and makes it the nearest Maugham ever came to writing a non-comic play successfully and seriously in the mould of the well-made play.

The Unknown, as I have said, is one of Maugham's few com-plete failures. Here he starts not from a pattern into which believable people may, with skill, believably be fitted, but from a couple of believable enough people who have to be fitted into a pattern. But in the fitting they became, if not necessarily less believable, at least less interesting as people. Maugham, as so often, put his finger on the play's principal drawback when he wrote:

The drama I saw in my mind's eye lay in the conflict between two persons who loved one another and were divided by the simple piety of the one and the lost faith of the other. But to my surprise, it appeared in representation that the drama lay in the arguments on the one side and the other and not at all in the personal relations of the characters. The result was that the play came to an end with the second act; the third consequently was meaningless, and there was no trick or device I could think of that could make it significant.

So, it seems to me, we must conclude that despite the real if qualified success of *Caesar's Wife* Maugham did not ever really achieve a decisive victory in the battle to reconcile the disciplines and requirements of the well-made play with the desire to write with high seriousness about the problems of real life in a way which gave an audience the illusion that it was seeing real life unmanipulated by a puppeteer, however masterly. It seems to me equally, though, that this is a question of personal limitation rather than a limitation inherent in the medium; it was not so much that it could not be done as that *he* could not do it.

But seriousness is not everything. Nor for that matter is high seriousness, tragic seriousness, the only way of being serious. In his three great comedies of modern manners, *Our Betters*, *The Circle* and *The Constant Wife*, Maugham constructs as brilliantly as in his lightest, most farcical works, and yet manages, indirectly and unobtrusively, to say more which is serious and to the point about the relations of men and women than he does in all his more solemn plays put together. In these three plays he reaches the high point of his art, and demonstrates himself one of the greatest comic dramatists in the history of the British stage.

The most involved of them, and certainly the most incident-packed, is *Our Betters*, which chronicles the progressive disillusionment of an impressionable American innocent with the way life is lived in Europe by her widowed sister and her friends, a group of rich, foolish American emigrés with their coterie of sugar-daddies, lovers, gigolos and miscellaneous hangers-on. It is all organized with the greatest skill and aplomb, but in *The Circle* and *The Constant Wife* Maugham had learnt to simplify his surface intrigue while enriching what lay beneath: they are, as Ravel said of his music, *complexes, mais pas compliquées*.

The Circle works by the ingenious superimposition of two parallel situations, thirty years apart. Arnold Champion-Cheney, an ambitious, priggish young politician, is embarrassed by the reunion in his house of his parents, in the presence of the lover with whom his mother ran off thirty years ago and has been living ever since. Meanwhile his own household is threatened with a similar crisis: his wife, understandably bored with him, is contemplating elopement with a romantic young planter about to return to Malaya. The plot of the play, after economically expounding these complications, resolves itself into disquisition on the question of whether the young can ever learn from the experiences of the old, and if so what precisely is there to be learnt in this case. Maugham later expressed himself as dissatisfied with the scheme Arnold's father suggests to him to keep his wife by emotional blackmail ('I should have liked at that point a more substantial and dramatic invention'), but in general the play was accepted at once as a triumph of wit and construction, and also of psychological realism: in it Maugham uses with consummate ease a deliberately artificial form to make some disarmingly true and sensible observations on life as it is really lived.

This use of the well-made play convention to enable the playwright to escape from limiting particularity into acceptable generalization is, if anything, even more marked in *The Constant Wife*. Its pivotal line comes near the end of the second act: Constance, after blandly assisting her husband and his mistress (about whose affair she is supposed to know nothing) to put the mistress's jealous husband off the scent, announces that she and her husband have been lucky, in that they were fortunate enough to fall out of love with each other simultaneously. From now on she will take a job, so as to be financially self-supporting and win the right, which she uses to devastating effect in the third act, to reproach him for his infidelity and repay him in kind. Again, the premises of the plot are unashamedly artificial; in particular the cigarette-case under the pillow which leads Anne-Marie's husband to suspect the worst is, as James Agate noted in his *Sunday Times* review, 'of a banality to make poor Scribe turn in his grave'. And yet it works here because it is so palpably an artificial device, a sort of dramatist's shorthand, to get the play on whither the author would have it go without the pointless and self-destructive labouring which would be needed to make the revelation seem natural and quotidian.

With *The Constant Wife* Maugham might reasonably think that he had carried his sort of theatre as far as he wanted it to go. Anyway, it seems that he did in fact think so, for shortly after its production he embarked on a strange and unexpected group of 'last plays' written entirely to please himself. He expected them to be unsuccessful, but felt that 'they would continue to pester me till I wrote them'. Surprisingly, and rather alarmingly, he includes *The Sacred Flame* among them. Were this not so one would have little hesitation in writing it off as a glib and efficient potboiler, virtually certain to obtain the commercial success it seems to court; in any case it is difficult to believe that Maugham himself could have taken it so seriously. The other three fit more understandably into the pattern of personal statement. For one thing, they all seem to go out of their way to convince the audience that they are not well-made, rather as though – which may perhaps be the case – Maugham had come to accept in his own mind that well-madeness and complete sincerity were incompatible, or – and let us hope more likely – that Maugham saw the three subjects as being ones which could not be readily dealt with in the confines of the well-made play, and therefore felt the gravest doubts about whether he could write them successfully, as he would have to, in a style foreign to his normal temperament and experience.

If this latter explanation is the correct one, it must be said at once that his forebodings were wrong about *The Bread-winner* and right about *For Services Rendered* and *Sheppey*. But then *The Breadwinner*, the only unarguable comedy of the three, is only at first glance not a well-made play. It is unique among Maugham's full-length plays in that the action is continuous, the intervals being introduced, according to the original programme, merely 'for the convenience of the audience.' It may therefore have seemed to Maugham something dangerously like an experiment in free form, but in fact if it is a rhapsody it is a beautifully coherent and, yes, well-made rhapsody. In its first section the themes are stated: the young, taking the security provided by their elders for granted, think their parents should be done away with at forty, while the elders, also complacent, cannot think that anything will seriously upset their way of life, even the fact that the one absentee may be about to be hammered on the Stock Exchange. In the second section all this is ironically reversed: the absentee, having returned, blandly announces that he will do nothing to save himself, accept no help; he is taking the opportunity to go off and make his own future without encumbrance. In the third section he receives unperturbed the varied reactions of his nearest and dearest, and at the last, with irreproachable human and dramatic logic, takes himself off alone, the breadwinner no more.

If *The Breadwinner* offended all its audience's conventional notions of duty and responsibility, at least it chimed in effectively with their secret desires, and anyway they could persuade themselves, for form's sake, that being a comedy it was all in fun. In *For Services Rendered*, though, this was not possible. The theme is similar: the urge to escape from duty, especially what other people impose on you as your duty, and to take what chances you have, however slim, of a life of your own. Maugham set out to write a harsh, true play, while recognizing how easily it might have been modified to achieve popularity – 'The characters had only to be sentimentalized a little to affect their behaviour at the crucial moments and everything might have ended happily. The audience could have walked out of the theatre feeling that war was a very unfortunate business, but notwithstanding God was in His Heaven and all was right with the world . . .' However, good, serious intentions do not necessarily make a good, serious play. The sufferings of the Ardsley family – mother dying of an incurable disease, son blinded in the war, one daughter unhappily married to a drunkard, another frustrated to the point of literal insanity, a third determined to run off with a married man she does not love just to escape, and at least one minor character disposed of by suicide just off-stage at the beginning of the third act – may represent some sort of truth, and a truth, at that, which Maugham felt at that moment an urgent personal need to state. But the play he wrote rambles and eventually descends into raging unintentional melodrama. And this time the blame cannot even be heaped on to the destructive influence of well-made-play conventions.

Sheppey, Maugham's theatrical swansong, is even more of a mystery. It is a weird and formless piece about a barber who wins the Irish Sweep and, in his family's view, goes mad in consequence, living literally according to Christ's teachings, giving away his money and taking into his house a prostitute and a thief (neither of whom likes it very much). In the end, and not before time as the other characters see it, he is called for by Death, in the guise of a beautiful woman, and goes off unwillingly, leaving what he conceives of as his work in the world largely undone. The play is disturbing, because it raises, as no other Maugham play does, the question of what he is trying to say. It seems to be a *pièce à thèse*, but the thesis, and even the theme, remain irritatingly elusive. When Pinero, in *The Enchanted Cottage*, tried to tackle a subject which depended for its effectiveness on suggestion and atmosphere, leaving questions to hang unasked, and certainly unanswered, on the air, he failed, for his was a technique apt above all for dealing with the clear-cut and precisely defined. In *Sheppey* Maugham makes the same attempt, and fails for the same reason.

Maugham himself put it another way. 'I grew conscious that I was no longer in touch with the public that patronizes the theatre. This happens in the end to most dramatists and they are wise to accept the warning. It is high time for them to retire.' And retire Maugham did; apart from taking a hand in the scripting of the film *Trio* (1950), based on three of his short stories, he wrote no more in dramatic form during the remaining thirty-two years of his long life. But by his success, commercial and artistic, he had reopened and kept open a case, that of the well-made play, which at the beginning of 1908 many, perhaps most, intelligent people connected with the British theatre imagined to be closed for ever. And, even more to the point, he wrote at least half a dozen comedies which stand with the best the English stage has to offer.

Barker, Galsworthy, Lonsdale

Pursuing Maugham's theatrical career to its end we have gone far beyond the 1900s. But now it is time to turn back and see just how the realistic well-made tradition fared in the years of Shaw's first great triumphs. For though Pinero and Henry Arthur Jones were already regarded as back-numbers, or about to become so, by the turn of the century, a way of writing drama which had proved so satisfactorily able to combine popular entertainment with a fair measure of critical esteem as serious literature could hardly be expected to vanish at once, even under Shaw's pyrotechnic barrage.

And indeed it did not. *Mrs Dane's Defence* left, for the perceptive, something of a challenge to be taken up. If the firmest old guard believer in dramatic and social conventions could suggest at the last that these interlinked forces in the theatre could be bolstered up only by lies and self-deceptions, it was obviously time that this English tradition should try at least to set its house in order on its own terms. These terms might owe something to Ibsen; might even owe something to Shaw. But more than that they were dictated by the forces of dissolution at work in the very heart of the well-made tradition, and before it succumbed to them completely a few dramatists thought it worth their while to put it to the test and see just how far it could go in the critical examination of its own basic premises.

One of the first to do so was St John Hankin (1869–1909), whose brief career in the theatre spanned only five years, from 1903 to 1908. Hankin's plays may not be the deepest or the most dazzlingly expert of their time, but they have a characteristic bitter flavour all their own and would be well worth some enterprising manager's while to rediscover. They use all the conventions of the well-made drawing-room drama à la Pinero, but are constructed entirely from the cynic's point of view, showing the social conventions within which their characters move not as ultimate truths in which everyone has to believe, but as rules in an elaborate game which can be manipulated at will by those cool and clever enough to use them for their own far from conventional ends.

The best of Hankin's work is to be found in the group which he defiantly called *Three Plays with Happy Endings: The Return of the Prodigal* (1905), *The Charity That Began at Home* (1906) and *The Cassilis Engagement* (1907). In *The Return of the Prodigal* the conventions are used by a 'waster' against his respectable, hard-working father and brother. He comes back from Australia after frittering away the £1,000 he was given to make a new start there, and cheerfully admits that he is extravagant, unscrupulous and entirely useless. So, his deadly secret is revealed at the outset, and the conventions that he should feel shame and repentance, and resolve gratefully to do better next time if he is given the chance, are entirely powerless against him. He can, however, use all the conventional notions of respectability and right-thinking against his family, and he does: they do not have to support him, of course, but if they refuse to what else can he do but go into the local workhouse? And how will that affect his father's dearly bought social position in the county, not to mention his chances of election to Parliament? His case is unanswerable, and the family gives in with what little grace it can muster.

The Charity That Began at Home is also an ironic comedy. Verreker, a free-thinker who believes in rational self-interest, falls in with a group of do-gooders, particularly a Lady Denison and her daughter Margery. He believes that their absurdly trusting generosity and all-purpose charity are a disease which should be wiped out for their own good; he also has the misfortune to fall in love with Margery. In an attempt to come to terms with the situation he spends a week trying to live life according to Margery's principles, but in the end, deciding that his selfish regard for his own happiness and his unselfish regard for Margery's happen fortuitously to coincide, he determined that he and Margery must separate, since once the passion of the moment has evaporated, what will there be left in common between them to sustain the long flat years of marriage?

The Cassilis Engagement carries Hankin's method a step further, and created something of a furore on its first production as the last word in iconclastic cynicism. It tells how a loving mother sets about breaking up her son's engagement to a common scheming girl she considers unsuitable not by opposing it but by apparently welcoming it with open arms. She invites the girl and her vulgar mother down to the country and gives them ample rope to hang themselves, relying on the supposition, quite correct as it proves, that they will spoil all their chances to be acceptable to the gentry and that faced with the boredom of aristocratic life as it really is rather than the splendid excitements cheap fiction has led them to expect, the fortune-hunters will soon cry off. The conventions as a liability which those not by tradition subject to them would do everything in their power to avoid – that was really turning the world of Jones and Pinero topsy-turvy.

It is difficult to guess – and pointless to try – what Hankin might have done in the theatre if he had lived longer. Maybe his ironical exploration of the well-made play's possibilities for self-parody would have been only a phase. Certainly well-made drawing-room drama was only a phase in the writing career of Harley Granville Barker (1877–1946). He did not begin realistically: the first play he wrote alone, *The Marrying of Anne Leete* (1901), is a lyrical celebration of the life force in which a young woman of gentle birth throws over all conventions and proposes to a gardener who has already been turned down by a local farmer's daughter in favour of the heroine's brother. The play veers between emotional drama and broad comedy, with a curious coda in which the oddly matched couple, alone in a cottage, tot up the risks they run in their search for happiness and decide that anyway the game is worth the candle.

But after this eccentric beginning Barker wrote three plays which are interesting in themselves and very much to the point at issue, in that they seem to be meant as well-made drawing-room dramas and yet constantly threaten to burst the form asunder. The first of them, *The Voysey Inheritance* (1905), deals with the family situation of the Voyseys, headed by a fine old rogue who has been gambling successfully for years with his clients' money. The play falls into two parts: the first, in which the relations between the various members of the family are presented, and the second, after the death of Mr Voysey senior, when his frauds are revealed and his main legatee, the self-righteous Edward Voysey, has to decide what to do about them. The troubles with the play are two-fold. The structure is anything but well-made: Pinero, no doubt, would have begun the play after Voysey senior's death, so as to avoid a broken-backed effect, but Barker has too many didactic ends in view to allow this, especially since it would prevent old Voysey from speaking for himself. And the story, as a story, has too many evident loose ends, depending too much on unforeseeable interventions (the revelation, the final debacle brought about by Booth) to advance and conclude it. The play, in fact, is primarily a talk-piece along Shavian lines, with each of the Voysey clan representing some particular attitude to life, and the attempts at a well-made realistic surface cannot disguise the basic unmanageability of such material in such terms.

Waste (1907) at least is simpler and more direct, and not so prodigal with its characters. Here the central situation is a confrontation between two people who think they love each other: Henry Trebell, an ambitious politician with an optimistic philosophy of life (the Life Force again), and Amy O'Connell, a pretty, silly Irish woman. For a while Trebell's enthusiasm and energy carry all before them, but when Amy finds she is to have a child she arranges for an abortion and dies on the operating table. The scandal ruins Trebell's career, allowing his ascetic adversary Cantelupe the upper hand and snatching a certain cabinet appointment from his grasp. The waste is Trebell's own career (he shoots himself), but also, and most of all, the waste involved in the foolish, unnecessary extinction of two lives, Amy's and the child's. Here the construction is clear, once the hurdle of a rather complicated and none too-clear exposition is over, but again the happenings are ever-increasingly subordinated to a mass of words while the characters explain exhaustively to themselves and everybody else what precisely is going through their minds.

The Madras House (1910) returns to the overloaded manner of *The Voysey Inheritance*, though by this time Voysey has gained considerably in technical skill and the exposition of the very complex physical and emotional set-up of the Huxtable establishment on Denmark Hill is conducted with consummate unobtrusive ease. Before long however everyone in sight starts talking his head off – especially Philip Madras, a nephew of the head of the house and son of the family's black sheep, Constantine Madras, a cheery hedonist who stands for everything the duty-bound Huxtables hate and fear. Philip is another of Barker's eager, searching, slightly priggish idealists, and as he gets into his stride on the subject of duty, narrowly defined, as a soul-destroying force, or expatiates to his wife on the necessity of moving out into the great wide world and taking up one's duty to humanity (in the first instance, by becoming a County Councillor!) the play gradually runs out of control.

Maybe Granville Barker was always too much the idealistic theoretician ever to make a practical dramatist: in 1902 Shaw wrote of him to Henry Arthur Jones, 'Do you realize that he is a great poet and dramatist who feels towards us as we feel towards Sheridan Knowles?' Certainly, though a great director of other people's plays he seemed to have some sort of blind spot when it came to his own, so eager was he that not one tiny point of their significance should be lost. Another hint of his uncertainty as a dramatist may perhaps be found in his unwillingness to let well alone: *The Voysey Inheritance* was elaborately revised twice, in 1913 and 1921, *The Madras House* once, in 1925, and *Waste* was completely rewritten in 1926. It is curious that he should have tried at all to embody his ideas in the form of well-made drawing-room dramas, and not perhaps surprising that for all his intelligence and theatrical experience he should have failed consistently to do so. In his later plays, anyway, he moved decisively away from drawing-room realism, so that his last two plays, *The Secret Life* (1923) and *His Majesty* (1928) verge on completely subjective fantasy, and in any case were written to be read rather than acted.

Compared with Granville Barker, John Galsworthy (1869–1933) gained considerably by being a distinguished man of letters as well as a prolific and successful dramatist. While Barker for some reason felt impelled to press all his ideas on life and society willy-nilly into the not necessarily suitable form of a play, Galsworthy was perfectly able, if he wanted to write a novel, to write a novel, and if he wanted to write a political pamphlet to write a political pamphlet. So, when he wanted to write a play, it was likely to be on a subject which he found most aptly treatable in dramatic terms. This was just as well, since aesthetically he was a dyed-in-the-wool conservative, and a play to him meant a play as the 1890s had understood it: a story with a beginning, a middle and an end, realistically conceived and written in the language really spoken by men, using as little artifice as possible and where it was not possible to avoid artifice (especially in the opening exposition) trying to conceal it as neatly as possible so as to avoid straining the audience's credulity. In addition, a play had, obviously, to be constructed, just like any other piece of literary craftsmanship: the parts must be in the right proportion to the whole, clear, logical continuity must be created and maintained, and no loose ends must be left dangling to irritate audiences. Also, Galsworthy believed passionately in truth: in the scrupulously fair presentation of both sides in any conflict, the undeviating arguing-out of any issue to its logical conclusion. And this, in his plays, was what he did.

That, in his best plays, he was able to achieve his aim so consistently is a tribute at once to his intelligence and to his considerable stagecraft. Dangers threaten from all sides: the temptation to over-simplify to make a point too quickly or neatly; the temptation to fall into overt didacticism. But in at least half-a-dozen major plays Galsworthy treads with admirable confidence and restraint the decent middle course. His is above all a theatre of decency, where fair-play and other gentlemanly virtues reign uppermost; and they, if unfashionable virtues, in the drama or anywhere else, are still by no means negligible.

In some of his early plays he does go so far as to signify, in the end, where his own sympathies lie; later, in plays like *The Skin Game* (1920) and *Loyalties* (1922), he balances his sympathies so evenly that there can be no suspicion that he has rigged things to favour one view or another. If we ask where our own sympathies should lie the only possible answer is, with everybody, suffering as they do in a fallen world.

But that suggests that Galsworthy's plays are high-flown, when their great advantage is their very prosaicness and down-to-earthness. They deal always in particular instances, and leave it to others to draw any general conclusions they may wish. The conclusions to be drawn from *The Silver Box* (1906) and *The Eldest Son* (1912) are perhaps obvious, but unexceptionable as a statement of fact: there is one law for the rich and another for the poor. In the first two thefts take place: a charwoman's husband steals a silver box from the home of an M.P. while bringing his son home drunk, and this same son steals a girl's purse while drunk. But the upshot of the two crimes is very different: influence and money see to it that all scandal about the upper-class young man's 'prank' is suppressed, but the charwoman's husband is brought to trial by due process of law and sentenced to a month's hard labour. In *The Eldest Son* a fine old English squire feels himself in duty bound to take a firm stand on moral principle when his under-gamekeeper gets a village girl into trouble and hesitates to marry her. On the other hand, when his own son does the same to a maid in the household he does everything in his power to prevent a marriage, even though in this case the boy is only too eager to marry the girl.

Justice (1910) is perhaps more of a *pièce à thèse*: there is no doubt that in writing it Galsworthy was eager, while carefully showing that no one administrator of the law and the prison system is necessarily malevolent, or indeed wishes for anything but the best for everybody, to demonstrate the inhumanity of the whole system within which they function. But even so the play is organized with scrupulous fairness. We are not asked to sympathize with the main sufferer, William Folder, because he is dashing and attractive, because he has special mitigating circumstances, or because he is the victim of a miscarriage of justice. On the contrary, he is a small, ineffectual and decidedly unattractive character, driven to his crime (forging a cheque) by nothing more admirable than a passion for a married woman, and undoubtedly he did commit the crime for which he is condemned. And yet by the end we sympathize with him just because he is a human being, however unprepossessing, and we feel that no one should be treated as he is. Incidentally, enough people felt so at the time for the play to be directly instrumental in bring about penal reforms.

Galsworthy's masterpiece of this early period in his dramatic work, and by general consent the most successful of all his plays, is *Strife* (1909), produced a year earlier than *Justice*. This is a monumental study of intransigence: the battle is between two idealists, Roberts, leader of the workers at a large tin-plate manufacturers, who has determined to fight for higher pay and better conditions and will brook no notion of compromise, and Anthony, chairman of the Board of Directors, who is equally certain that he is right not to give in to any of their demands. On both sides there are those eager or willing to compromise, but the matter is in the hands of Roberts and Anthony, the irresistible force and the irremovable object. The result is a strike in which everybody suffers, not least Roberts, whose wife dies because of it, and in the end both leaders are faced with rebellion among their own followers. A compromise is reached – the same one which was worked out by more moderate forces in the union and the company to begin with. No good has been done to anyone, and 'the two best men both broken'. But that, as the trade unionist remarks bitterly at the final curtain, is 'where the fun comes in'.

As a dramatic progression *Strife* yields nothing to Sardou, while in intelligence it matches Shaw, only to excel him in high seriousness. Galsworthy never quite equalled this again, but his gifts did not desert him and he had the prestige to ride out changes of fashion in the theatre, remaining true to his original canons of theatrical craft right into the 1920s. In many ways *The Skin Game* and *Loyalties* are anachronisms, but anachronisms of amazing vitality. Both present dramas turning on a conflict which is in its essence unresolvable between two rootedly opposed views of life – very much after the pattern of *Strife*. In *The Skin Game* it is a battle between two families for control of a piece of land which each of them, for all sorts of reasons, creditable and discreditable, is determined to wrest from the other. On the one side are the Hillcrests, landed, cultivated, somewhat effete and sufficiently removed from go-getting ancestors who elevated them to command neither the power nor the money they once did. And on the other are the Hornblowers, the new go-getters, brash, vulgar, mercenary, but at the same time willing to pay for their place in the sun, convinced, properly enough, that they have earned it, willing to learn from the old guard and stung to understandable irritation by the ill-bred snobbery of the squirearchy. Both start in a fairly honourable position, both stop at nothing to achieve their purposes, and if this time it is Hornblower who is ultimately the loser there is no knowing how the contest might turn out on another occasion. And certainly what the Hillcrests think they are fighting for – the integrity of their England – looks dangerously compromised by the means they use to preserve it – shameless blackmail based on the shady past of Hornblower's daughter-in-law.

In *Loyalties* the conflict in the first place is between Captain Ronald Dancy and Ferdinand de Levis, one an aristocratic officer, the other a rich Jew, who happen to be guests together, over the week-end, at a country house. De Levis is robbed, and accuses Dancy of the crime. The host and the General cannot believe that an officer and a gentleman could be a thief, and so take his side and warn de Levis not to repeat his story. He, however, regards their attitude as simply a closing of aristocratic ranks brought about by anti-Semitism, so he deliberately repeats his accusation in the club both he and Dancy belong to. Here the club committee are torn two ways by conflicting loyalties, and arbitrate that the two men involved must go to law to decide. It looks as though Dancy, aided by his lawyer, an old friend, will win, until unexpected evidence comes into the lawyer's hands that Dancy is in fact guilty. His loyalty towards the law wins out over his loyalty to his friend, and he withdraws from the case. Faced at last with discovery and ruin, Dancy shoots himself. And who, in all this, is most deserving of sympathy? Galsworthy leaves it entirely up to us to decide – he just tells the story, and abstains from comment of any sort.

Both these plays were successes in an era which already seemed to have turned its back finally on the old-fashioned problem play, the drawing-room drama and anything which seemed to savour of stuffy convention. *Loyalties* was produced in the same year as Noël Coward's *The Young Idea*; they must have seemed to belong to two different worlds. Galsworthy, by now shaping as a Grand Old Man, went on writing, and still, occasionally plays; he even, in *Escape* (1926), tried to make an unexpected break with his own tradition and wrote a play constructed quasi-cinematically in a succession of short scenes in ever-changing locales as his principal character, an escaped convict, desperately sought shelter and safety.

But for the moment *Loyalties* sounded very much like the death-knell of the old drama. Serious theatre was heading off in a dozen different directions at once, and none of them much concerned with old-time craftsmanship or even, except for a few energetic attempts at regional drama in Manchester, with detailed surface realism. Gordon Craig's theories of a new dynamic, non-realistic theatre in which the actor and the writer would take their proper place as tools in the all-powerful director-creator's hands might not have had much direct effect at home, but new ideas of stagecraft crept in from abroad. And new writers too. The Irish literary renaissance threw up Synge and Yeats, with their different concepts of poetic theatre, and rather later produced Sean O'Casey. Russia sent Chekhov's free, lyrical, atmospheric plays, obtrusively lacking in 'construction', and, to complicate matters further, the totally subjective dramas of Andreiev. In Germany then was Expressionism, in France the exquisitely stylized productions of Copeau at the Vieux Colombier. Even at home there was something of a revival in verse drama, there were the enormously successful fantasies of J. M. Barrie, and there was, always and ever, George Bernard Shaw.

However, there was still one area in which the well-made play still held its own: in light comedy and farce. Even there its grip might seem momentarily to be slackening: one of the most spectacular comedy successes of the era was the succession of Aldwych comedies written by Ben Travers between 1925 and 1933. And Travers, while anything but a technical primitive – his autobiography, *Vale of Laughter*, is a positive textbook of laughter-creating techniques – was by no means an adherent of the well-made play. Plays like *Cuckoo in the Nest* (1925), *Rookery Nook* (1926) and *Thark* (1927) ramble all over the place, picking up and dropping characters without rhyme or reason, the perfect dramatic embodiment of an era which prided itself on believing that anything went.

Still urbanity was not altogether dead in comedy. Its principal champion in the early 1920s, when Noël Coward still looked like an anarchic rebel, was as it happened someone rather unlikely, Frederick Lonsdale (1881–1954). Unlikely because up until the production of *Aren't We All?* in 1923 he had been one of the most consistently popular dramatists of the London stage, but almost exclusively as a provider of books for musical comedies, a genre noted in general for neither its wit nor its formal coherence. Who would have expected that the author of *The King of Cadonia* (1905), *The Balkan Princess* (1910), *The Maid of the Mountains* (1917), *Monsieur Beaucaire* (1919) and *The Lady of the Rose* (1922) would turn his hand instead to high comedy and take up where Wilde and Maugham left off? As it happens there might have been a few people: those who had seen his very modestly successful comedy *The Best People* in 1909 – *Aren't We All?* was a rewritten version of it – or who had read another play of his, *The Follies of the Foolish*, when it failed to get produced in 1904 – that later turned up rewritten as *On Approval*.

But for most *Aren't We All?* was a bolt from the blue. Its plot is about as slight as one could imagine, its centrepiece being our old friend from the Nineties a Woman with a Secret. In this case she is a young wife who comes hurrying back from Egypt to find her husband in the arms of another woman. She is righteously indignant, but her husband's father has a weapon to use in his efforts to restore her to a more charitable frame of mind: he finds out that the reason she returned so speedily was because in Egypt she found herself on the verge of falling into precisely the same trap as her husband. Armed with this knowledge he sets about a bit of moral blackmail; his daughter-in-law responds to his plotting by trapping him into marriage with a woman he has been evading for years. So one way and another everything turns out very much for the best in this only mildly cynical view of the world.

The plot, as I say, is little or nothing. What distinguishes Lonsdale is his extreme dexterity in keeping his audience guessing, so that though they may safely rely on what will eventually happen they never know from one minute to the next exactly how it is to be brought about. And covering the whole proceedings in glitter-dust is Lonsdale's dialogue, a model, it has been said, of 'dialogue which, though not lifelike, is apparently lifelike.' It could also be said that there is much in Lonsdale's dialogue that seems like wit but is not wit. For rudeness, we are always told, is not wit. And undoubtedly many of the best effects, the funniest lines in Lonsdale are based on rudeness. But rudeness exercised with such consummate ease and nonchalance, such immaculate timing and pointing that it becomes almost an art-form in its own right. And with such maniac single-mindedness and conviction that our belief in these extravagant creatures and their extravagant words never wavers; we simply accept that in such very special circumstances these very special people could talk this way – indeed, could not possibly talk otherwise.

Two years later Lonsdale's biggest success, *The Last of Mrs Cheyney*, appeared. The title deliberately suggests the Nineties – *The Second Mrs Tanqueray*, *The Notorious Mrs Ebbsmith*, *Mrs Dane's Defence* – but this time the eponymous heroine has not only a shady past but an even shadier present and future. Though masquerading in London society as an Australian lady of some position and means, and already being wooed by two variously-intended noblemen, she is really, as comes out at the end of the first act, part of a gang of jewel thieves. In the second act she sets about putting into effect her plan to rob her hostess, Mrs Ebley, of her pearls during a country week-end. But one of her suitors recognizes a member of the gang, intercepts a message which discloses the plan, and arranges an excuse to change rooms with Mrs Ebley. So, when Mrs Cheyney arrives in Mrs Ebley's room, she finds Lord Dilling waiting for her. He offers to let her escape if she will give him what he wants first. She refuses and rouses the house; moreover, when he tries to smooth things over she announces the truth and leaves the party in a state of scandalized confusion. In Act Three they debate over breakfast what to do with her until her other suitor tells them that in a letter of proposal to her he included remarks about those in society he could not have her associate with (i.e. themselves) which could cause many red faces if made public. Consequently, the tables are turned, with all her fellow-guests offering to buy her off for £10,000. She agrees, but then tears up the cheque and tells them that she has already torn up the letter that morning. As they leave, we learn that she has decided to opt for respectability from now on, and is about to become Lady Dilling.

The fusion of high comedy and detective drama was novel and yet comforting; audiences knew where they were, which, for all the play's intriguing backstairs details about how the rich and titled live, was clearly cloud-cuckooland. *On Approval* (1927) was even further removed. It is a four-character play taking place largely in a remote Scottish shooting-box where Maria Wislack, an egotistic and imperious widow of uncertain age, takes her easy-going, well-meaning suitor Richard on a sort of trial marriage to see how they suit each other. Along for the ride, as it were, and also to decide how they suit each other, are an equally obnoxious, egotistic and quite penniless duke and his inamorata, an immensely rich pickle heiress. They manage to get isolated, servantless, and set gleefully about savaging each other until the worms finally turn and leave Maria and the Duke of Bristol to rend each other directly without convenient butts to vent their spleen on. It is the culmination of Lonsdale's comedy of rudeness; the refinements of insult and recrimination indulged in by the widow and the duke are calculated with incomparable finesse, demonstrating that if rudeness is not necessarily wit, at least in the hands of a master it may consistently attain to that desirable state. *On Approval* is Lonsdale's most sustained *tour de force* of comic writing; and the peak of his career.

His last play of the 1920s, *Canaries Sometimes Sing* (1929), rounds out Lonsdale's quartet of classic comedies. Again it isolated four characters in a country house. This time they are two ill-assorted married couples who go through a complicated pattern of changing and re-changing partners as the charms and disadvantages of first one character then another become apparent, until in the end three of the four are exposed as the convention-bound bores they are and the heroine, Elma, goes off hopefully to look for 'another co-respondent', leaving the rest to their fate. After this Lonsdale had only one failure produced in London until 1944, and though his last three plays, *Another Love Story* (1943–44), *But for the Grace of God* (1946) and *The Way Things Go* (1950) were all commercial successes only the last recaptured anything much of the old magic. Still, during the 1920s he did keep the flag of high comedy flying, and stood as the champion of Edwardian urbanity against the rowdy rebellion of youngsters like Noël Coward. Of course in historical perspective things seldom seem as distinct and clear-cut as they did at the time. . . .

Noël Coward

When a new full-length play by Noël Coward, *A Song at Twilight*, opened in London early in 1966, the author was surprised, he afterwards admitted, to find that not only was it on the whole favourably reviewed, but that in general the most favourable reviews came from the youngest and allegedly most iconoclastic critics. On consideration, though, there is little real cause for surprise; this was Coward's thirty-third full-length play to be produced (that is, leaving out of account more than a dozen one-act and half a dozen revues). The older critics had grown up with Coward as one of the fixtures of the West End stage, recognized but not subject as a rule to close examination. The younger critics, on the other hand, had been busy during the year or two previously with rediscovering Coward as a classic, via revivals of *Private Lives, Present Laughter, Blithe Spirit* (even in a rather shaky musical adaptation) and *Hay Fever* – this last enshrined at the National Theatre.

Looked at with eyes of wonder, *A Song at Twilight* is indeed a remarkable phenomenon in the theatre of 1966: a straightforward well-made play such as Pinero would have thoroughly approved, but with a mid-century twist in that its subject proves, in a splendidly attention-grabbing first act curtain, to be the homosexual past of a well-known author. The story, despite its novelty-value and its topicality (evidently posthumous revelations about the private life of Somerset Maugham must have played some part in its elaboration), is thinnish, and what most excited favourable critics, I think, was the extreme skill with which it is told. Not a trick in the handbook of play construction is missed. The opening exposition, telling us about the writer's present marriage and his famous liaison with a star actress in the past, is a model of how to do these things as painlessly as possible, and get us eagerly awaiting the arrival of the actress, now paying the author a visit after many years apart. The actress arrives, the game starts in earnest, with a devious to-and-fro over their precise relationship in the past and whether he will or will not let her publish his letters to her in her memoirs (shades here of Shaw and Mrs Patrick Campbell). And so, as their tempers worsen, we get to the first-act curtain, with the revelation that the writer has been for much of his life, whatever the façade he chose to present, a practising homosexual.

That is certainly, even in 1966, ending an act with a bang, especially in the plushy, restful surroundings of an all-star evening sponsored by H. M. Tennent. The bang is fair enough, too: on reflection, we decide, perhaps Latymer was a trifle too admiring of the waiter's shoulders to be altogether above suspicion. But it is the sort of bang which creates problems when the curtain goes up again, for once the first shock of the revelation is over, how do things go on without anti-climax? There again Coward has all the cunning of a master-craftsman. While luring us on with details of Latymer's history and disastrous relationship with a completely impossible man, he gradually starts tipping the scales in the other direction. Now that the actress has played her trump card, what does she hope to win? The right to publish the letters? Is that the point of her blackmailing threat to publish other, more compromising letters in retaliation? Perhaps, but it is not enough. Her basic feeling is that Latymer has cheated – himself as much as anyone, and as a result of that, the world, since even his writings have been affected by his living a lie. What she seems to want is some sort of admission from him, some sign that he has under-stood. And in the middle of this emotional tug-of-war, Laty-mer's present wife returns, to help disarm the poor man completely, by showing him how few secrets he has left, for all his care about keeping them.

It is a wrily ironic conclusion, which sends the audience out of the theatre satisfied that the movement initiated at the outset has been completed, but at the same time leaves enough ques-tions hanging in the air to make them think a little. For instance, though nobody has a good word to say for Latymer – not even himself, really – the question remains of whether he does not have something to be said in his favour that cannot be said of either of the women in the play – that he has felt real passion at least once in his life, and has suffered because of it, while both the women seem to be theorizing in a vacuum. It is not, doubtless, a particularly deep play, but it is not either a facile or an un-intelligent play. It is, in other words, a good well-made play – hence all the excitement and the praise, in this, our own post-Brecht, post-Beckett era.

So, one might think, the old master can still do what he has always done. But that is not quite an accurate picture of the place *A Song at Twilight* occupies in Noël Coward's work. Rather, it marks the closing of a circle. For what we tend to forget today is that Coward, now the old master of the classical tradition in English drama, has not always been, or been taken to be, the obvious logical successor of the well-made-play tradition. On the contrary: in his early days he was regarded as a young revolutionary, all too ready and eager to throw out of the window everything which Pinero, say, would have thought most important in drama. If *The Vortex* now seems to us in most ways – and especially in technique – a thoroughly conservative play, in 1924 it looked very different. (It is interesting to remember that another, comparable play considered revolutionary in its time, *Look Back in Anger*, also seemed to its author a few years after the event to be 'a formal, rather old-fashioned play'.)

And the revolutionary quality critics and audience detected in the early works of Noël Coward were by no means entirely a matter of the subjects he treated (an unhealthy relationship between mother and son, gleeful and shameless adultery indulged in by nice middle-class wives, etc). His technique too was considered revolutionary, precisely because it went right against the canons of the well-made play in one particular. Well-madeness was originally – as viewed by Sardou for instance – not so much having a neat plot as having a lot of plot and telling it in such a way that the audience's interest was never allowed to flag. The French farce-writers refined this in many ways, by harnessing the mass of plot material to a rigid symmetrical frame, but still the amount of plot, the proliferation of incident, was vital. The decisive step Noël Coward took here, whether in comedy or drama, was a drastic lightening of the plot-load.

A characteristic early Coward play has far less plot, far less incident, than a Pinero play or even a Maugham play. What plot there is is handled in a fairly traditional manner – as Maugham remarks in his graceful and amusing introduction to Coward's *Bitter-Sweet and Other Plays* (1929), 'in his construction he has been content to use the current method of the day' – but instead of being the solid walls of the play it tends to become a skeleton framework merely. This means that Coward's plays, in comparison with those of his immediate predecessors on the English theatre scene, appear lightweight, because they choose to be so; Coward recognized that the architectural analogy for play-making was false, because a play is in performance – and his plays are above all plays for performance – an experience in time. So, returning to the origin of the well-made play, he accepts wholeheartedly Scribe's initial sleight-of-hand approach, stripping away all the accretions of later, more solemn dramatists.

This might be taken to mean that his plays, while perfectly acceptable as 'mere' entertainment, are strictly for the moment, and not worth a critic's time and trouble. In fact this is just the conclusion which many critics did reach, especially in the big dip Coward's reputation took in the 1950s. But now here are a number of the once looked-down-on plays popping up as good and fresh as ever when most of their weightier, more seriously meant contemporaries are clearly dead as a doornail. How to explain this? First, I suppose that the well-made play had been tending to become more and more literary, further and further from the ordinary theatrical experience. This happens here and there even to Pinero, and even more, whatever may be said in their favour, in the plays of such distinguished men of letters as Harley Granville Barker and John Galsworthy. Now the one thing that no one has ever denied Coward's plays is that they are of the theatre, theatrical. To read them one might think there was nothing there, but put them on stage and they immediately – the best of them anyway – spring to life. Sleight-of-hand one may call it that they get so far with, apparently, so little; but it would be more realistic to regard Coward's method rather as a perfectly just estimation of what does and does not work in the theatre: there is no point in bringing a heavy barrage to bear on something which a scattering of buckshot can move with perfect efficiency.

So, Noël Coward's plays got by with a minimum of plot. But this is not the only way in which they are lightened. There is, too, his highly personal way with dialogue. Maugham, in the introduction already quoted, puts it in a characteristically teasing, double-edged way.

It is in his dialogue that Mr Coward has shown himself something of an innovator . . . he has deliberately avoided the epigram that was the fashion thirty years ago . . . and has written dialogue that is strictly faithful to fact. It does not only represent everyday language, but reproduces it. No one has carried naturalistic dialogue further than he. . . . It was inevitable that some dramatist should eventually write dialogue that exactly copied the average talk, with its hesitations, mumbling and repetitions, and broken sentences, of average people. I do not suppose anyone can ever do this with more brilliant accuracy than Mr Coward. My only objection to it is that it adds greatly to the difficulty of the author's task. It is evident that when he represents dull and stupid people they will be as stupid and dull on the stage as they are in real life and they will bore us in the same way. When he exposes his theme or joins together the various parts of his story (and I should think it was impossible to write a play in which certain explanations, of no interest in themselves, can be avoided) he will only with difficulty hold the attention of his audience. The author limits himself to characters who are in themselves exciting or amusing and to a theme which is from the beginning of the first act to the end of the last naturally absorbing. It is asking a great deal. I may point out in passing that as Ibsen's dialogue grew more naturalistic he was led to deal with singularly abnormal characters. . . . Now that naturalistic dialogue has been carried as far as it can go, I cannot but think it might be worth trying a dialogue which does not reproduce the conversation of the day and only very vaguely represents it. And since the future of the English drama is in the hands of Mr Noël Coward this . . . with my blessing, is the suggestion I offer him.

Excellent and sensible, so far as it goes, though one cannot help wondering whether extreme naturalism of dialogue is quite the first thing which would strike the modern reader about *Bitter-Sweet, Hay Fever* and *Easy Virtue*, the three plays Maugham was specifically introducing. Of course, naturalism is in the eye of the beholder, and naturalism as understood in 1929 would necessarily be something rather different from naturalism as understood in the mid 1960s, both equally being conventions dependent for their acceptance on many factors quite outside drama. But whether we think that Coward's dialogue in the 1920s is naturalistic or not, it is evident that the convention in which he wrote dialogue at this period was, or was felt to be, something radically different from what had gone before.

Again, if we examine the question in detail, it is obvious that what Coward was doing was reforming the well-made-play tradition to take out some of the literature which had been imported and put back, not necessarily more real life, but certainly more theatrical life. And this depends first and foremost on a clear realization that plays are not primarily, perhaps not even significantly, for reading, but for speaking. So dramatic dialogue can afford to drop a lot of what would be necessary in something meant just to be read. The actors are there, and their tone of voice, their comportment towards each other, even their facial expressions can convey a lot which therefore does not need to be spelt out in words. This is not necessarily an observation based on real life, but simply a statement of theatrical fact; and in the same way Coward's dialogue is not as it is because he has observed how people in real life speak and has copied them, but because he has observed what works most effectively in the theatre and what does not. Indeed, when Maugham argues with the Coward view of dramatic dialogue – as he interprets it – because it does not take sufficient account of the literariness with which many people, especially the educated, speak and suggests that 'stage dialogue has been simplified out of relation with all life but that of the cocktail bar,' he is within reach of the proper point, but coming at it, as it were, from the wrong direction. Of course people do not speak as clearly and economically as they do in a vintage Coward play. That is precisely where his art comes in – by expressing so much with such an economy of means.

Let us take a concrete example: the famous reunion scene between Elyot and Amanda, once married, now divorced and remarried to two other people, in *Private Lives*. They meet again while on their respective honeymoons, and find that for all the bad blood there has been between them they are curiously uninclined to leave each other and go back to their respective spouses.

ELYOT: It's shameful, shameful of us.

AMANDA: Don't: I feel terrible. Don't leave me for a minute, I shall go mad if you do. We won't talk about ourselves any more, we'll talk about outside things, anything you like, only just don't leave me until I've pulled myself together.

ELYOT: Very well. (*There is a dead silence.*)

AMANDA: What have you been doing lately? During these last years?

ELYOT: Travelling about. I went round the world, you know, after –

AMANDA (*hurriedly*): Yes, yes, I know. How was it?

ELYOT: The world?

AMANDA: Yes.

ELYOT: Oh, highly enjoyable.

AMANDA: China must be very interesting.

ELYOT: Very big, China.

AMANDA: And Japan –

ELYOT: Very small.

AMANDA: Did you eat sharks' fins, and take your shoes off, and use chopsticks and everything?

ELYOT: Practically everything.

AMANDA: And India, the burning Ghars, or Ghats, or whatever they are, and the Taj Mahal. How was the Taj Mahal?

ELYOT (*looking at her*): Unbelievable, a sort of dream.

AMANDA: That was the moonlight I expect, you must have seen it in the moonlight.

ELYOT (*never taking his eyes off her face*): Yes, moonlight is cruelly deceptive.

AMANDA: And it didn't look like a biscuit box, did it? I've always felt that it might.

ELYOT (*quietly*): Darling, darling, I love you so.

AMANDA: And I do hope you met a sacred elephant. They're lint white I believe, and very, very sweet.

ELYOT: I've never loved anyone else for an instant.

AMANDA (*raising her hand feebly in protest*): No, no, you mustn't – Elyot – stop.

ELYOT: You love me, too, don't you? There's no doubt about it anywhere, is there?

AMANDA: No, no doubt anywhere.

Naturalistic? Hardly. But that is an unimportant technicality. More to the point is to observe how it works. Literarily there is almost nothing there – the lightest, slightest persiflage. And yet much more is conveyed than at first appears. In the context of performance we not only listen to what is said, and laugh, as intended, but we understand what is being thought while the words are said: we understand that what is really happening in this scene is something quite other than what is being said. In effect, two people hopelessly in love with each other are busy trying to maintain the fiction that they are not, that they converse like ordinary strangers about ordinary matters – a pretence bound inevitably to break down sooner or later. This is an effect new in the context of the well-made play, where dramatists have tended to say what they mean and mean no more than what they say; but it is more in the nature of a reformation than a revolution.

To find out exactly how this reformation came about, and how Noël Coward came by 1929 to be recognized (by Maugham again) as the writer in the English theatre exerting most 'influence with young writers', so that 'it is probably his inclination and practice that will be responsible for the manner in which plays will be written during the next twenty years,' we must look in some more detail at his début and early career. He was born in Teddington in 1899 and after various amateur experience as a performer made his first professional appearance at the age of eleven in a children's play called *The Goldfish*. He began writing lyrics and composing songs in his teens, and had written two unpublished novels by the time he was nineteen. In 1918 he wrote his first play, *The Last Trick*, a four-act melodrama. It was turned down, amiably, by the impresario Gilbert Miller, who said that the dialogue was good but the construction lousy, and passed on the thought that 'the construction of a play was as important as the foundations of a house, whereas dialogue, however good, could only at best be considered as interior decoration.'

The result of this was the immediate composition of three plays, one of which, *The Rat Trap*, was Coward's earliest-written play to reach production, though not till 1926. It is not worth any very serious consideration; again, it is a melodrama, concerning the emotional ups and downs of a couple of writers who have the misfortune to be married to each other. The quarrel scenes between them are, as Coward himself observes in his autobiography, rather good, and the rest shakily put together, leading to an improbably lame and sentimental conclusion, when the couple come together again because she is having a baby. This was followed in 1919 by something a little more characteristic, a light comedy called *I'll Leave It to You*, which Coward wrote from an original idea by Gilbert Miller, about a family aroused from their lethargy by the promise of a legacy (nonexistent, as it turns out) to whichever of them shall have succeeded best in making good. Still the tone is uncertain: the construction depends too much on the element of suspense set up by a single question in the audience's mind, and the dialogue, though bright and brittle, still suggests more of Pinero in light-hearted mood than of the cocktail-twenties.

But already the first piece of 'typical Coward' was just around the corner: *The Young Idea*, a 'comedy of youth' written in 1921 and first performed in 1922. Here the tone is deliberately, self-consciously modern, and the theme one which was to become obsessive in the 1920s, the intricate and delicate rela-

tions between generations. The first act establishes that George
Brent's second wife Cicely is having an affair with a friend,
Roddy, that George does not mind so long as she is discreet,
and that he has two teenage children by a previous marriage,
with advanced ideas of their own. In the second act the children,
on a visit from living with their mother in Italy, plot to dispose
of Cicely and bring their parents together again; the first part
of their plan works when they manage to precipitate Cicely's
elopement with Roddy. The third act introduces an American
suitor for the mother but then eliminates him and gets the
parents together again, by final curtain.

Though in certain respects the play is derivative, particularly
in what concerns the characters of the children Sholto and
Gerda, who are very evidently, as Coward has admitted, based
on Dolly and Philip in Shaw's *You Never Can Tell*, it has
enough originality to justify Shaw's own judgement, that this
young man might make a good playwright provided he never
again read any Shaw. For at the same time it is, despite a
certain strain of riddling and paradoxical humour, a remarkably
un-Shavian play. Significant, no doubt, that *You Never Can Tell*
should be the ostensible model, for that is one of Shaw's closest
approaches to a well-made traditional farce – farce somewhat
humanized, admittedly, but still using the settings, props and
character-stereotypes familiar in the theatre of the time. One
can, indeed, imagine Coward learning little of use to him in
the development of his own talents from any other Shaw play,
and it perhaps tells us more about Coward and about this
Shaw play in particular than it does about Shaw in general that
You Never Can Tell should be the avowed starting point of
The Young Idea.

Except for a certain obtrusive casualness about extra-marital
relations, *The Young Idea* is not in any marked sense extravagantly different from the plays of Maugham or even the farces
of Pinero. The established materials are given a fresh and
personal twist, simply because the author has his own highly
individual voice. But there is little here to alarm even the most
conservative playgoer of 1922: the connections with what had
gone before are clear to see. Even so, the lightening process I

have remarked on, the trimming and skimming of the well-made play to remove all excess of 'literature', was already started. It continues in the sequence of comedies Coward wrote at intervals in the next eight years, most notably *Fallen Angels* (1923), *Hay Fever* (1924) and *Private Lives* (1929). Before we come on to these, though, it may be a good idea to look a little more closely at the dramas he wrote during the same period, particularly *The Vortex* (1923), the play above all which established Coward in the theatre of his time as an important and, specifically, a revolutionary, iconoclastic young writer.

The Vortex, for all its *succès de scandale* on its first production, is a thoroughly backward-looking play. The trappings of its plot may belong to the Twenties – the jazz and the mah-jong, the fashionable vocabulary of the characters – but when we look more closely it soon becomes evident that the technique and construction are essentially those of Pinero. James Agate, when reviewing the first production, very properly remarked that while the play was 'the *dernier cri* in the theatrical mode' at the same time its 'craftsmanship is beyond reproach, and the dialogue is taut and spare, and of an admirable *vraisemblance*'. He found 'the first act . . . a-shimmer with wit of the best theatrical kind – the non-literary sort that has to be spoken in the situation' (here Coward's lightening of the well-made play's machinery was clearly in evidence) but otherwise is in no doubt, and leaves us in no doubt, that whatever the decoration this remains under it all a thoroughly respectable, workmanlike piece of well-made theatre. In this he saw more clearly than most, who were in the main bowled over uncritically by the 'excessive modernity' of the whole proceedings.

Just how traditional the layout of the plot is may be seen at once in a brief summary. The first act starts with exposition unashamed: two friends of the heroine discuss in her absence, and thereby inform us of, her current affair with a man young enough to be her son, and in fact exactly the same age as her son. The stage thus set, interest is aroused in what will happen next by some dark warnings from one of the friends, Helen, to the heroine, Florence, and by the unexpected arrival of Florence's son Nicky from Paris, with the news that he is engaged and that the girl will be arriving forthwith. This she does, and Florence causes further consternation by apparently welcoming her instead of opposing the match as expected. As the curtain falls Buntie, the girl, and Tom, Florence's lover, discover they were childhood friends, and Nicky at once evinces jealousy. All this is done with the greatest technical fluency and ease. The opening explanatory conversation is disguised with great cunning as character-revelation: we discover only later, if we ever consciously remember to note it, that the two friends, Helen and Pauncey, are in fact lay figures, present almost entirely to tell us things we would not otherwise know. The various other pieces of the puzzle, including the one allowable major coincidence, the previous acquaintance of Tom and Buntie, fall effortlessly into place in an extended scene which plants each tantalizing clue to future developments with the clockwork inevitability of a classic chess match.

Having thus raveled his plot, all the dramatist has to do is to unravel it. The second act consists of a series of rows arising from the seeds of discord planted in the first act. Nicky has a brief flare-up with Helen over what later proves to be her recognition that he takes drugs. Florence squabbles with Tom. Nicky quarrels with Florence about Buntie, having already quarrelled with Buntie at the end of the previous act. As a result of all this Buntie breaks off her engagement with Nicky, and then for a grand finale Nicky and Florence find Buntie and Tom in each others' arms, so that the act can end with Florence begging Tom to come back while Nicky pounds thunderously on the piano.

Act Three ties up the loose ends. Tom and Buntie are gone, and it is time for the great confrontation of Nicky and his mother. This is done, quite deliberately, as a sort of modern-dress equivalent of the closet scene in *Hamlet*. Nicky attempts to bring Florence face to face with her own shallowness and emptiness, and finally succeeds in doing so, or appearing to do so, when the revelation that Nicky takes drugs persuades Florence that she must help him before it is too late; they must help each other. To do this she must promise to give up her lovers as he promises to give up drugs – and on this satisfyingly moral note, with both principals in tears and on the verge of hysteria, the curtain descends.

It does not sound like a very profound or, in its implications, a very believable conclusion. And no more it is. We may choose, as Agate did having once disposed of the required moralizing tag about how 'nauseating' the creatures of the dramatist's imagination are, to take the conclusion as merely a momentary respite: the next day they will both go back to their old ways, and it is only for the moment that they can convince themselves that they have at last and for good seen the light. But Coward does not give us any reason within the play for supposing this, whatever he may presume our sophisticated minds are likely to tell us in the foyer. The ending as it stands is surefire theatre: no less, but certainly no more.

And this is where *The Vortex* falls short of, say, *His House in Order*. Pinero, however melodramatic his presuppositions, has a certain dogged persistence in reasoning his way through to a conclusion which makes some sense beyond the instant theatrical effect. Coward does not do this in *The Vortex*, but makes do instead with an ingenious but palpable piece of theatrical sleight-of-hand. And as such it works, works superbly. But only at the expense of any pretensions Coward might have to be a dramatic thinker. One obvious answer to this is that Coward has no pretensions to being a dramatic thinker anyway, but has set out quite deliberately to write lightweight entertainments which pass our time agreeably in the theatre and leave not a wrack behind. This is possible, and yet somehow most of *The Vortex*, up to the middle of the last act anyway, does not give quite that impression. More to the point perhaps, is the possibility that in this play, form – the given, well-made-play mould – is at war with what he wants to say, and in the end wins, with the untidiness of reality sacrificed to a thumping good melodramatic curtain.

Certainly from the rest of Coward's works I believe this to be so. For Coward at the time of *The Vortex* seems to have reached that point where, even though for the time being no better formula offered, or none anyway that a writer bent on success as a commercial playwright could reasonably contemplate, the onslaughts of Shaw on the well-made play had done their work. Confidence – except for a rooted conservative like Galsworthy – had been lost in the well-made play as a vehicle for serious writing in the theatre. For comedy the conventions were perfectly acceptable: the existence of Shaw did not, after all, preclude the existence of Somerset Maugham – they simply inhabited two different spheres of theatre. Coward could write completely without damaging self-consciousness in the well-made play form as long as he was writing comedy; but in serious drama the battle was lost even before it was joined.

This perhaps explains why, for much of his career since *The Vortex*, Coward has tended to steer clear of any hint of the well-made play when he has wanted to say something seriously on the stage. Which is not the same thing as saying something serious: *Private Lives* and *Design for Living* are fundamentally as serious as any twentieth-century British plays, even though they choose to say what they have to say in comedy form. Perhaps, again, it is just that Coward is one of those writers who most naturally express themselves in comedy; and yet for all his brilliance as a comedy writer it does not seem so. One cannot help wondering, anyway, if this would have been the case had he been born a generation or two earlier, when he could have written well-made dramas without the haunting suspicion that the form might be inherently inadequate as a vehicle for serious ideas.

However, it is rather pointless to spend much time considering how far personal temperament and how far the mood of the time went to determine the bias Coward's career would follow; it is enough to note that it has followed a fairly consistent pattern from the earliest days up to the present. And that pattern is a rigid divide between his well-made plays, which are generally funny, and his plays in freer forms, which are generally serious or sentimental. Before the divide is completely opened, however, Coward wrote one play, *Easy Virtue* (1924), about the plight of a mysterious woman with a past in the stuffy upper middle-class country home of her second husband's family, which constitutes something of a deliberate farewell to the well-made play as Pinero knew it, and has the added interest of having inspired Coward to one of his few extended notes on his relationship with the drama of the immediate past, in the introduction to the relevant volume of his collected plays:

> From the 'eighties onwards until the outbreak of the 1914–18 War the London theatre was enriched by a series of plays, notably by Somerset Maugham or Arthur Pinero, which were described as 'drawing-room dramas'. I suppose that the apotheosis of these was *The Second Mrs Tanqueray*, but there were many others; *Mid-Channel, Lady Frederick, The Notorious Mrs Ebbsmith, His House in Order, Jack Straw, The Tenth Man, Smith*, etc., etc. There were also the more specialized Oscar Wilde comedy-dramas and the too infrequent, beautifully constructed plays of Haddon Chambers.
>
> All of these 'drawing-room dramas' dealt with the psychological and social problems of the upper middle classes. The characters in them were, as a general rule, wealthy, well-bred, articulate and motivated by the exigencies of the world to which they belonged. This world was snobbish, conventional, polite, and limited by its own codes and rules of behaviour, and it was the contravention of these codes and rules – to our eyes so foolish and old-fashioned – that supplied the dramatic content of most of the plays that I have mentioned. The heroine of *His House in Order* rebelled against the narrow pomposities of the family into which she had married. Lady Frederick, by gallantly and daringly exposing the secrets of her dressing-table, deflected the attentions of a young man who was infatuated by her into a more suitable alliance. In a recent revival of the play, this scene still proved to be dramatically impeccable. The unhappy Paula Tanqueray tried valiantly to live down her earlier moral turpitude, but ultimately gave up the struggle and perished off-stage in an aura of righteous atonement just before the final curtain. It is easy nowadays to laugh at these vanished moral attitudes, but they were poignant enough in their time because they were true. Those high-toned drawing-room histrionics are over and done with. Women with pasts today receive far more enthusiastic social recognition than women without pasts. The narrow-mindedness, the moral righteousness, and the over-rigid social codes have disappeared, but with them

has gone much that was graceful, well-behaved, and endearing. It was in a mood of nostalgic regret at the decline of such conventions that I wrote *Easy Virtue*. When it was produced, several critics triumphantly pounced on the fact that the play was similar in form and tone and plot to the plays of Pinero. I myself was unimpressed by their perception, for the form and plot of a Pinero play was exactly what I had tried to achieve.

In these remarks he comes near to saying in so many words exactly why the well-made play had ceased in his view to be a satisfactory vehicle for serious social drama; he also hints at, without directly acknowledging, the reasons why *Easy Virtue* is not finally a very satisfactory play. These are, precisely, the author's consciousness that patterns of behaviour have changed and his eagerness to show how they have changed. The well-made drawing-room drama was above all a theatrical pattern based on a social pattern; essential to its effect was the imaginative presence of a rigid convention of behaviour against which everything done by anyone (in certain classes, at least) would always be measured and judged. This is present for the Mrs Tanquerays and Ebbsmiths, and even in certain respects for Maugham's Lady Fredericks and Constant Wives, in the same way that the concept of honour is always present in Corneille. But when that convention is lost or broken, as it is for Coward's heroine Larita Whittaker, then the form crumbles too. The revelation about Larita's past, which should come pat on cue, remains arbitrary and implausible, and exotic motivations have to be found for behaviour (especially that of Larita's hot/cold, neurotically religious sister-in-law) which would have been thought perfectly natural and even proper in the 1890s. The last act, which should crown the previous two, is prevented from doing so, and from seeming anything but anticlimactic, just because people don't have things out like that in 1924; the big social dramas end not with a bang but a whimper. *Easy Virtue* is really an attempt to write a well-made drama about the impossibility of writing well-made dramas any more, and gets broken, or at least badly torn, on the horns of its own dilemma.

And after *Easy Virtue* Coward's non-comic ventures, right up until *A Song at Twilight*, are consistent in just one thing; their avoidance of evident well-madeness. Not so his comedies, however: here his natural inclination towards meticulously neat plotting and crystal-clear articulation of parts could be given full rein. And so we have *Fallen Angels, Hay Fever, Private Lives*, and after them *Design for Living* (1932), *Present Laughter* (1939), *Blithe Spirit* (1941), and a number of lesser works, dwindling down to *Nude with Violin* (1954). They are all basically sex-comedies, as perhaps they must be in a world where, socially, anything goes: the recurrent theme is the romantic triangle, complicated and reinterpreted in various ways, and the recurrent setting is a separate world in which clever, witty, extravagantly articulate people can step aside to cultivate their own emotional gardens free from such tiresome distractions as having to earn a living. In Wilde's comedies, and even in Maugham's, we are kept conscious of the great world outside the drawing-room, and of the repercussions it may have on what goes on inside. But Coward's drawing-rooms are nurseries where overgrown children can take refuge, safe from the world, to play at being grown-ups for as long as they care to and on exactly what terms they choose. Significantly there are no real children in this world, marriages are always childless unless the children are old enough to count already as adults.

This divorce from certain aspects of everyday reality might be considered, and indeed often has been considered, a crucial weakness in Coward's comedies. And yet they remain obstinately alive when, if they were really as flimsy as they are said to be, they should have vanished long ago. The answer, perhaps, is that their abstraction from the everyday world is merely a convention which permits them to examine the subject-matter they choose to examine with more concentration and intensity than would otherwise be possible. The emotional entanglements of their characters are presented in a pure form, without any distracting irrelevancies, just as, in a very different register, are those of Racine's characters; plots are reduced to the lightest possible framework, verbal show is always kept in check by the requirements of the situation, so that the funniest lines are funny only in context. In this Coward's comedies, for all their evident relationship with the whole well-made play tradition, are truly modern: they travel fast, get straight to the point, and carry no excess baggage.

Each play presents a group of people who find it impossible to live together and impossible to live apart. In *Fallen Angels* it is two young wives who spend a riotous, miserable evening waiting to entertain a Frenchman, at various times the lover of both, and each of them determined that come what may, the other shall not have him alone. In *Hay Fever* the triangles interlock: an extravagantly theatrical family entertain for the week-end, each one of them, father, mother, son and daughter, bringing a potential lover who promptly gets involved with some other member of the family. But again the nursery wins out – in the end all the interlopers are routed while the family closes in on itself, shut in its own private world. *Private Lives*, of course, is about a couple who have divorced because they cannot live with each other, get together again (though both remarried) because they cannot live without each other, then nearly split up again only to decide in the end that their world of private fantasy, whatever its drawbacks, is still infinitely more satisfactory than any feasible substitute. *Design for Living* carries the argument a stage further: it is about two men and one woman who find, by an elaborate process of trial and error, breakings-up and regroupings, that really their lives are satisfactory only when the three of them are together in their own cosy little world. *Present Laughter* is another play about theatricals, particularly Garry Essendine, a fortyish actor whose life revolves in small circles with a group of intimates to look after him and a number of girls who just wander in and out, the whole thing being unobtrusively stage-managed by his separated wife Liz. Again there are various triangle situations involving an *ingénue* would-be-actress, the knowing wife of Garry's best friend, the best friend, Garry's agent, and an over-eager hero-worshipping playwright with a thing about Garry. And again it is all resolved with a return to first principles: Garry goes back to Liz, since nanny always knows best. *Blithe*

Spirit is yet another triangle: this time a man with two wives, one alive and one dead but persistently present as a ghost to complicate things.

It would be silly to attempt to philosophize these plays into something they are not and were never meant to be. They are, obviously, what Allardyce Nicoll consents to call *Blithe Spirit* 'a minor comic masterpiece of the lighter sort'. And yet there is something more to them than mere persiflage, a series of lines which, as Congreve said of Cibber, 'seem like wit and are not'. And that something more is, for want of a better term, human interest. Coward's spectrum of humanity may be limited, it may confine itself to a very small section of society in a very small range of emotional entanglements, but within that range he is a complete master. However extravagant their behaviour, his comic creations do live as people and their lives go on behind and under and around what they are saying: the text provides only the faintest guidelines to what is really going on between the people on the stage.

And curiously enough, it has not been the critics who have noticed this – critics have generally echoed the patronage of Allardyce Nicolls's comments in *World Drama* ('amusing no doubt, yet hardly moving farther below the surface than a paper boat in a bath-tub, and, like the paper boat, ever in imminent danger of becoming a shapeless, sodden mass'). It has been dramatists above all who have seen how Coward's plays really work, and have learnt from it. The names of Harold Pinter, Henry Livings and Ann Jellicoe may seem unlikely as figurants in study of Coward, yet they are the ones who have commented most perceptively on the art of Noël Coward and seen him, not as the fustiest of the old fogies, but as in a very vital sense the father of them all, the great exemplar of a British 'drama of the unspoken' in which thoughts speak louder than words.

After this it is something of a let-down to come back to Coward's later work outside comedy. He has dabbled in all sorts of forms, several of which – the revues and musicals, the one-act plays – need hardly concern us. The romantic dramas which find their expression largely in music – *Bitter-Sweet*,

Conversation Piece, Operette – are organized as loosely as such shows generally are, and even the musical-comedies proper like *Sail Away* make full use of the musical's formal liberty. It is difficult at this distance of time to take *Cavalcade,* Coward's through-the-years patriotic spectacle of 1931, much more seriously, and indeed to judge by Coward's own comments in the introduction to *Play Parade* Volume 1 he never took it very seriously either, though he singles out two scenes, the funeral of Queen Victoria and the outbreak of war in 1914, as well-written. More interesting are Coward's two dramas connected with the Second World War, *This Happy Breed* (actually written in 1939 but not produced till 1942), which mirrors the history of the inter-war years in a rambling chronicle of one working-class family's life in one house in Clapham, and *Peace in Our Time* (1946), a rather similarly organized attempt to present a panoramic picture of Britain under five years of supposed German occupation through a series of happenings in the saloon bar of the Shy Gazelle, somewhere between Sloane Square and Knightsbridge. Both plays are unashamedly episodic, and mix sentiment, melodrama and a bit of comic relief with some adroitness, if little of lasting moment.

During the 1950s Noël Coward continued to write, mainly comedy, and London saw in succession *Relative Values, Quadrille, South Sea Bubble* and *Nude with Violin,* none of them up to his best and *Nude with Violin,* a farce about a deceased painter who did not, as it turns out, paint any of his pictures, tailing off into something very near his worst. Two adaptations, *After the Ball* and *Look After Lulu,* were hardly more successful, but technically interesting. *After the Ball,* a musical version of *Lady Windermere's Fan,* in the event told us little about Coward the dramatist *vis-à-vis* Wilde, since it foundered on the almost unsolvable problem of how to integrate musical numbers into a perfectly satisfactory and workable stage play (albeit no masterpiece) without slowing everything down alarmingly. *Look After Lulu,* on the other hand, being a translation-adaptation of Feydeau's *Occupe-toi d'Amélie,* told us quite a lot about Coward's relations with classic French boulevard farce. The whole trouble was that, in line with his own comedies, he tried to humanize the play: taking an original in which character beyond clear farcical stereotype is non-existent and verbal wit entirely subordinate to the precise manœuvrings of the plot, he inserted epigrams and attempted to develop the characters of the luscious but unreliable Lulu and her host of exotic admirers into rounded comedy creations. The result was disastrous – the fabric of the play was just torn apart. And yet at least it confirms one thing: that Noël Coward, even when he wants to, cannot be wholly confined to a paper boat in a bathtub.

And so full circle to Noël Coward's two latest full-length straight plays, *Waiting in the Wings* and *A Song at Twilight*. One of them, *Waiting in the Wings*, is perhaps his most completely satisfactory attempt at a completely free form: a tragi-comic picture of life in a home for old actresses (another nursery-surrogate, perhaps?), it covers a few months in four independent scenes, each satisfactory as an independent episode and yet all reinforcing each other to create a beautifully light, well-balanced whole. There seems to be no organization at all, and yet Coward when taxed with this rejects the idea that the play marks his eventual triumph in free form: 'I could take you through that text and show exactly how each part fits into a tight overall construction,' he says, and no doubt he is right. But at least he has finally written a play which is not a comedy, not to all appearances a well-made play (no matter how meticulously it may be constructed according to its own lights) and which yet works with perfect confidence at a level deeper than immediate theatrical effectiveness.

A Song at Twilight, at the other end of the scale, is a serious drama (with, admittedly, its moments of barbed comedy) which takes up the form of the well-made play *à la* Pinero and uses that with complete mastery, thinking its characters with impeccable logic through a succession of revelations to a conclusion which does not, for once, step aside into facile theatricalism. It stands with Rattigan's *Man and Boy* as the first completely convincing, completely serious well-made play in the British theatre for more than half a century: since Galsworthy's *Loyalties*. It is strange that both plays should concern them-

NOËL COWARD

selves, in part, with the question of homosexuality. Maybe the new leniency of the Lord Chamberlain on this subject has opened a new field of subject-matter for social drama, in which as in few other areas of our modern sexual and social mores, there is a clear line of convention drawn against which all behaviour can be and almost inevitably is measured. Or maybe not; maybe it is a pure coincidence. At any rate, it is surprising and not a little cheering that in his sixties Noël Coward, still sprightly and improbable for the grand old man role in which he has been cast, should still be progressing, still meeting the perennial technical challenges of his theatre with new resources. There can be few dramatists nearing seventy of whom it can still be said that one really has no idea what to expect of them next.

Terence Rattigan

As the 1930s succeeded the 1920s it became increasingly obvious that the most remarkable thing about British drama in the twentieth century was to be how little it was affected by changing times. Waves of dramatic rebellion might rush in one by one, but they broke in vain at the foot of the white cliffs, and British dramatists remained in general wedded to the pre-dominantly realistic theatre of their fathers and grandfathers. But with, unfortunately, a failure of conviction: they might not change so much, but they were painfully conscious of change about them, and found whole-hearted adherence to the old canons of the well-made drawing-room drama impossible. So what emerged tended to be something betwixt and between: modified realism, loose and untidy construction in the work of dramatists like James Bridie who found it impossible to emulate the merits of Shaw without taking on at the same time even more of his faults.

Perhaps the dramatist of the 1930s who most clearly suggested in his work that something new might be coming was T. S. Eliot (1888–1965), but this mainly by being and staying completely outside the traditions of the current commercial theatre with his non-realistic verse plays *Murder in the Cathedral* (1935) and *The Family Reunion* (1939). Oddly enough in the three successors to these he wrote after the war, *The Cocktail Party* (1949), *The Confidential Clerk* (1953) and *The Elder Statesman* (1958), he seemed bent, superficially at least, on reintegrating himself: though they were all written in verse, it was verse so unnotice-able as such that the unprepared listener might take it for prose, and the forms in which the plays were written might at first glance be taken respectively for drawing-room comedy, farce in the *Importance of Being Earnest* style, and problem drama.

However, classical origins to the stories lurked obscurely, and the author's designs on us were manifestly very different from those of the commercial dramatists whose superficial mannerisms he chose to adopt.

Two other dramatists of the 1930s who had something personal to offer were J. B. Priestley (born 1894) and Emlyn Williams (born 1905). Priestley came to the theatre by first of all adapting, in collaboration, his own novel *The Good Companions* in 1931. Then in the next eight years he wrote sixteen plays. Stylistically he is thoroughly eclectic, ranging from the basic North Country farce of *When We Are Married* (1938) to the completely non-realistic allegory of *Johnson Over Jordan* (1939). Somewhere in between came the plays most germane to our purpose, the 'time plays' *Dangerous Corner* (1932), *Time and the Conways* (1937), *I Have Been Here Before* (1937) and *An Inspector Calls* (1945) in which he attempts to revitalize the drawing-room drama by infusions of a mysterious alternative reality, another plane of being which owes much in its imaginative elaboration to the theoretical writings of the philosophers J. W. Dunne and Ouspensky about the nature of time. In each the comfortable, familiar atmosphere of a stage drawing-room is broken by the intrusion of something strange and intangible: a 'dangerous corner' in conversation which is turned the first time but smoothly passed by the second; a feeling that 'Some things that happen for the first time Seem to be happening again', with the attendant possibility that we may be able to change what seems to be their predestined course; a person from another world, another time-scale perhaps, who brings to us uncomfortable truths we would rather not know.

These plays at least show a serious attempt to come to grips with the problem of realism in the modern theatre; Emlyn Williams's best plays act as though the problem did not exist. His thrillers like *A Murder Has Been Arranged* (1930), *Night Must Fall* (1935) and *Someone Waiting* (1953) work excellently on their chosen level, particularly the second. His Welsh-whimsical pieces survive less well, and his most lasting play may well prove to be a semi-autobiographical piece, *The Corn is Green* (1938), in which he tells in gentle, realistic terms the story of the decisive influence brought to bear on a young Welshman's future by a Welsh schoolmistress who encourages him to read and go to university. But this, if realistic, is scarcely well-made; elsewhere his plays, if well-made, are scarcely realistic. For using to the full the license English critics have always been ready to permit the Celts in matters of eloquence, Emlyn Williams developed his own sort of primarily rhetorical theatre free from the self-consciousness which dogged his soberer English contemporaries.

But the well-made tradition, if universally taken for dead, just would not lie down. As we have seen, Noël Coward, seen at the time as the leading rebel against all that it stood for in the English theatre, proves in retrospect to be its most powerful upholder, once he has lightened and reshaped the tradition to suit his own style and way with a story. Terence Rattigan (born 1911) carried things a step further. His first one-man effort, and one of the most spectacular successes of his whole spectacularly successful career, was *French Without Tears* (1936), a comedy even lighter than Coward's. It has virtually no plot: there are three young men and one not so young cramming French on the Riviera: Diana, the sister of one of them, is along for the ride, a *femme fatale* alternately adored and detested by the other three; and there is a pretty French girl secretly in love with one of Diana's adorers who, unknown to himself, is really in love with her. Diana flirts with one swain then another, and ends up in headlong pursuit of a third, the member of the party up to now most seemingly immune from her charms. Jacqueline, the other girl, picks up the man of her choice on the rebound.

And that is that. There are no complications, nothing in the dialogue which could even remotely pass for epigram. The whole thing works, in fact, on the cunning with which the various characters are moved around, brought into unexpected collision or unlikely coalition; the comedy is, under the bright, bustling surface, a gentle comedy of character, in which each seems for a moment to be faced with what he has most desired and finds that it is in fact what he most fears. The framework

seems fine-spun, but it is really surprisingly firm, and if any-
body had bothered to do more than laugh at the play – which,
understandably, at the time no one did – he might have won-
dered if it was not, as well as being a remarkably confident
first solo run, a cheering promise of something more substantial
to come.

For a while it hardly seemed so. Three years later Rattigan's
next play, *After the Dance* (1939) had little success with either
critics or public, and two succeeding collaborations did not get
anywhere. Rattigan has not seen fit to preserve *After the Dance*
in print: it was apparently about a pair of superannuated once-
bright young things whose life of quiet drinking and desperation is interrupted by a ruthless young reformer, a girl who
drives Joan, the wife, to suicide (in the middle of a party)
and sets the husband David to work again with a good dose
of strict discipline. It sounds as though it might be rather
interesting, with many incidental possibilities for the drama of
degradation and humiliation which has been recurrent in
Rattigan's later work. Also, somewhat to our point, at least
one critic, in *The Times*, evoked the shade of Sardou to suggest
the way Joan's suicide worked and the extent to which, for
him, it did not work.

So by 1942 *French Without Tears* was six years behind and
its record run (1,049 performances) was beginning to look like
a flash in the pan. Then came something entirely different:
Flare Path, a wartime drama of life in the R.A.F. and specifically
life for the women the fliers left behind. The play was craftsmanlike and timely. The three parallel love stories, of an
ex-actress torn between her husband, a bomber pilot, and her
old flame, an American film star who needs her, a sergeant's
wife whose grumbling at everyday irritations obscures her real
love for her husband, and a barmaid married to a Polish count
she believes will be through with her once the war is over, are
managed with some resource, and the climax in which the
actress chooses duty rather than love and the barmaid learns
at last, in a classic letter-reading scene, just how much she
meant to her husband, hits the audience without scruple in
their softest and most sentimental area. Perhaps the play does

not, now, seem to have much truth, but it is ineffably of its period and a thoroughly expert piece of popular play-making. So was its successor, *While the Sun Shines* (1943), an adroit farce about three men in one flat, an ordinary-seaman duke, a Free-French officer and an American officer, and the duke's fiancée who becomes incidentally involved with the other two when the American mistakes her for one of the duke's former girl-friends. That ran even longer than *French Without Tears* (1,154 performances, to be precise) and then vanished leaving hardly a trace in the memory.

Rattigan's next comedy, *Love in Idleness* (1944, retitled *O Mistress Mine* in New York) shows some real advance: written for the Lunts, it plays a Hamlet-like situation neatly for laughs. The son in this case is a seventeen-year-old brought up in Canada, who returns to London to find his mother involved with a married man, the Canadian-born Minister of Tank Production. Since he is full of left-wing convictions, as well as the more personal reactions sons are supposed to feel in such circumstances, he takes to lecturing everyone about their failings and provides his elders with something of a problem. The problem is all worked out quite neatly, and the play for all its bright surface has at times a note of genuine feeling which gives it distinction.

But for all that *The Winslow Boy* (1946) came as a complete surprise. For what it is, quite deliberately, is a full-dress revival of the well-made drawing-room drama, with a secret which is finally revealed and a big *scène à faire* leading up to a dramatic reversal at curtain-time: not only does it recall the Archer-Shee case of 1908, but it does so in dramatic terms much closer to those of *Mrs Dane's Defence* than anything since. A cadet at the Royal Naval College is accused of stealing a 5s. postal order and expelled. His father believes him when he says he is innocent and sets out to fight the case. When approaches to the Admiralty and an attack through his M.P. get nowhere he engages a famous K.C., Sir Robert Morton, to handle the case. The big scene is the confrontation between Sir Robert and Ronnie Winslow, the boy, in which Sir Robert cross-questions and browbeats Ronnie until it seems that he must be convinced of the boy's guilt, and then calmly announces that he will take the case, since the boy is plainly innocent. As a result of his activities in Parliament a Petition of Right is granted and the case can be fought in the courts. The Winslow family meantime suffer: the daughter's engagement is broken off, the elder son leaves Oxford and their savings are whittled away. But in the end Ronnie is vindicated and there is a suggestion of romance between Sir Robert and Catherine, the suffragette daughter.

It is an intelligent, well-written play: terms which in themselves have come to sound rather patronizing. There is no need to patronize *The Winslow Boy*, though: it is a good evening's theatre in the old style, it tells a strong story well, and in the role of Sir Robert Morton it creates a not unbelievable figure, a 'cold-blooded, supercilious fish' who yet has at least one passion – for justice, and even more, for the 'right' which a Petition of Right requires to be done. All this is a lot, certainly, and yet some reservations remain. The play is, as I have said, a deliberate, self-conscious piece of revivalism: not only a period piece in its materials, but a period piece in the way they are put together. It is a fascinating technical exercise, and one which seems to have served Rattigan well in his subsequent work, when the scrupulous concern for shape has been less immediately obvious but not less importantly present. It has always been something of a paradox that while the playwright whose plays are not well-made often does everything in his power to make them seem so, those whose plays are well-made tend to do all they can to conceal the fact. And Rattigan is no exception: having demonstrated in *The Winslow Boy* his ability to meet the dramatists of the 1890s on their own terms, in the plays which come later he can take his constructive powers for granted. But as for *The Winslow Boy*, it remains for me somewhat flawed as a play by its very effectiveness as a demonstration: because this sort of well-made problem play would not come naturally to a dramatist in 1946, would not that is be his unthinking way of expressing himself in theatrical terms, it has for all its merits the slight stiffness and mechanical quality of a test piece, admirable but not really impassioned.

The fruits of the disciplines Rattigan imposed on himself are immediately apparent in his next substantial work, a long one-act play *The Browning Version* (1948). This is beautifully shaped, but unobtrusively so. It is a portrait of a schoolmaster, Andrew Crocker-Harris, on the point of retirement after eighteen years of unsuccessful teaching in which he has failed entirely to convey his love of the classics to any of his pupils and has merely got himself the reputation of being 'the Himmler of the lower Fifth'. His marriage too is on the rocks: his wife, frustrated and dissatisfied, has turned to another man who is now about to discard her, and her attitude towards Crocker-Harris is one of vicious destructiveness. The climactic moment of the play is that in which a small boy, Taplow, gives Crocker-Harris a second-hand copy of Browning's translation of the *Agamemnon* of Aeschylus, his favourite play. This small gesture unleashes the pent-up emotions of half a lifetime, and even though Crocker-Harris's wife tries to spoil it for him, by suggesting that the book is merely a sweetener to avoid punishment, at least the feeling that he may have got through to just one of his pupils gives him the courage to make one small gesture: he will after all say a few words of farewell at the end-of-year assembly.

The Browning Version, as well as being at once Rattigan's tightest and most natural-seeming construction job up to then and his most deeply felt play, marks the beginning of his most distinctive and personal drama. It brings to the centre of his stage two subjects which are to recur with variations and developments throughout his work: humiliation, already an important part of *The Winslow Boy*, and the role of the neurotic, embittered dissatisfied woman in life. Millie Crocker-Harris is the first of a line, the first sketch of a character who turns up again, immediately recognizable, in *The Deep Blue Sea, Separate Tables, Variation on a Theme* and even *Nelson: A Portrait in Miniature*.

Before he returned to the emotional world of *The Browning Version* in *The Deep Blue Sea*, however, Rattigan wrote two lighter-weight works. The first, *Adventure Story* (1949) seems in principle one of his most ambitious plays: a large-scale historical drama on the life of Alexander the Great. It is clean, clear and efficient, scaling down the characters to easily recognizable human terms and saying a number of interesting things about them. All perfectly creditable, in fact, but hardly compelling. The second, a comedy called *Who is Sylvia?* (1950), nobody seems to like much, though I have always had a soft spot for it. It is the light-hearted story of a quest for an erotic ideal: the Sylvia whom Mark, aristocrat and diplomat, was attracted to in boyhood and continues to look for in various women throughout his life. The play is loosely put together: in effect it is a series of one-act plays with the same central character and following much the same pattern, taking place in 1917, 1929 and 1950, and topped off by a final appearance of the wife who has known what he was up to all these years and let him be. Slight and rather silly, it charms by its little touches, as with the Sylvia-surrogate who when offered caviare refuses gracefully with 'I never did care much for *fishy* things' – a perfect example of the Rattigan line which is irresistibly funny in its character context, where it counts for the play, but means little anywhere else.

The Deep Blue Sea (1952) was generally regarded at the time of its appearance as Rattigan's best play, and if he has arguably written better since it remains, with *Man and Boy*, the play in which he has most happily constructed a fully articulated plot according to well-made principles without too obviously showing his hand. The play starts with a splendidly attention-grabbing situation: the heroine unconscious after an attempt at suicide has been foiled when the meter in her seedy, oppressive flat has cut off the gas. Why did she do it? That is what the play sets out, with cunning indirection, to show us.

Hester is married to one man, a judge who seems pleasant, civilized and understanding, and living with another, a flier who, if not the greatest intellect in the world, is obviously amiable and devoted to her. And yet she is not satisfied. She is a thwarted idealist, in search of a sort of ideal, all-consuming love which neither can give her. During the day we see just how both of them have failed her, or, to put it another, fairer way, how she has failed and goes on failing to comes to terms with life.

The husband offended her by treating her as one of his possessions, a desirable decoration for his elegant home in Eaton
Square; the lover, a hearty man's man, loves her according to
his lights but does not begin to understand her – his real life is
elsewhere, with the chaps at the pub or on the golf course,
around cars and planes, and though he knows that something
is radically wrong at home he has not the faintest comprehen-
sion of what it is or how to put it right. Both men, anyway,
regard Hester's demands on them and on life as impossible,
and of course they are right: Hester is really a silly woman
with no internal resources whatever, asking for no less than
that she should be able to centre her life entirely on a man whose
life will be entirely centred on her. All escape routes seem to be
barred, and at the end, after the progressive revelations of
incomprehension and incompatibility, she is left one spiral
further down, nearer that deep blue sea which, when you
find yourself between it and any devil, can begin to look so
dangerously inviting.

The great advantage of the play is that, given three main
characters who are in various ways mentally and emotionally
crippled, Rattigan manages to understand them, and make us
understand them, to a point where all achieve a measure of our
sympathy: all mean well and do their best in a situation which
has no easy way out, and perhaps no way out at all. In particular
he manages beautifully the character of Freddie, the lover. In
French Without Tears this exchange occurs:

KIT: I wonder what it's like to be as hearty as Brian?
JACQUELINE: Awful, I should think.
KIT: No, I should think very pleasant. Have you ever seen
Brian bad-tempered?
JACQUELINE: No, but then I think he's too stupid to be bad-
tempered.
KIT: It doesn't follow. Cats and dogs are bad-tempered, some-
times. No, Brian may be stupid but he's right-minded. He's
solved the problem of living better than any of us.

An intellectual's idealized view of the noble savage, perhaps,
but with a measure of truth in it. In the character of Freddie,
Rattigan sets out to explore just how far that truth extends, and

in doing so makes real and believable a type of man who in the theatre has usually been left, like Brian in *French Without Tears*, as a comic stereotype. The scene in which Freddie tries to explain to a friend what he feels about Hester and the whole impossible situation he has walked into is one of the subtlest and most precisely observed in the whole of Rattigan's work. After *The Deep Blue Sea* came some more light-weight pieces. *The Sleeping Prince* (1953) is a slight and amusing fantasy about an elusive amatory encounter between a sophisticated European prince and a charmingly naïve showgirl, with the prince's handsome son intervening. In *The Final Test* (1954) Rattigan first ventured into television, having already written original scripts for various films, most notably *The Way to the Stars* (1945) and *The Sound Barrier* (1952). *Separate Tables* (1954) was another new departure: a pair of one-act plays linked by locale (both take place in the same seaside private hotel) and by the fact that the principal roles in each were taken by the same actor and actress. One of the stories, involving two estranged sophisticates and their edgy reunion, was conventional and unmemorable, but the other, about the involvement of a faded, aging spinster terrorized by her gorgon-like mother and a phony military man whose pathetic deceptions are revealed when he is accused of interfering with a woman in a cinema (before censorship, of accosting men in a lavatory), has some sharp observation and again manages to make characters out of people who are usually in the theatre left as mere comic caricatures. The heroine of the first play, incidentally, presents another facet of Rattigan's destructively neurotic female, while the second is entirely about humiliation, and the kinship the humiliated may find with each other.

Separate Tables, in fact, marks the beginning of a phase in Rattigan's career which has excluded comedy almost entirely: apart from an ill-advised and short-lived musical version of *French Without Tears*, *Joie de Vivre* (1960), all Rattigan's plays since have been dark and often bitter. In *Variation on a Theme* (1958) the 'theme' might be interpreted in two senses: literally it is a harshly ironic rehandling of *La Dame aux Camélias*; in terms of Rattigan's own work it is a field-day for his typical heroine. Rose Fish, much married, and the richer by each husband, is presented as the modern equivalent of the *grande cocotte*, who marries her men instead of merely being kept by them. At the start of the play she is on the verge of marrying for a fifth time; she is also suffering from tuberculosis, *à la* Marguerite Gautier. But meanwhile she allows herself to become involved with an empty-headed, unscrupulous ballet-dancer with the temperament of a tart: he is on the make as much as she ever was, and rather more blatantly. One bust-up persuades her to get rid of him, but then she changes her mind and ends by setting off with him for one last mad spree instead of retiring to a sanatorium for the treatment necessary to save her life.

The play offers a couple of showy central roles for an aging actress and a beautiful young man, but it suffers from some uncertainty of tone, with Rattigan trying to have his cake and eat it, to send up the romantic melodrama implicit in Dumas fils while at the same time relying on it to work seriously when it can serve his theatrical purpose. Also the character of Rose obstinately refuses to come into focus. Partly, perhaps, this comes from Rattigan's divided purpose, but there are as well various signs – the hints of homosexuality in the boy's background, the more central role homosexuality plays in Rattigan's next two stage plays – which make one wonder if Rose is not essentially a male character forced to go *en travesti* by the Lord Chamberlain's censorship regulations at the time.

Rattigan's next stage play, anyhow, marked a complete change of pace. *Ross* (1960) is best seen in the line of *Adventure Story*, though this time it concerns recent history: the strange career of T. E. Lawrence, Lawrence of Arabia. The construction is tighter than in *Adventure Story*: Lawrence's adventures in the desert are framed by scenes in which he, now disguised as an unknown soldier, reflects back on the fame and the degradation from which he is now not very successfully (and perhaps not very convincingly) trying to escape. But still the construction is freer and more episodic than Rattigan has normally permitted himself, maybe because his dramatization of Lawrence's story began as a script for a projected large-scale film which succumbed to one of the British cinema's recurrent economic crises. For the central episode which provides the key to Lawrence's character Rattigan chooses, as one might expect, the major humiliation of Lawrence's life, when he was captured by the Bey of Deraa, refused (according to his own published account, anyway) the Bey's homosexual advances and was then flogged to breaking point before making his escape when the Bey, who had all along taken him to be a Circassian, refused him as 'a thing too torn and bloody for his bed'. Rattigan interprets this episode as a turning-point in Lawrence's life, in which he was forced to face the truth about his own nature, the limits of his self-control, and once having done so began to die of the knowledge. It may not be the true explanation, or the complete explanation of Lawrence's later career, but it is as likely as any, and makes excellent dramatic sense, as does the barbed relationship between Lawrence and Allenby which provides a sardonic background to Lawrence's showier military exploits.

The Final Test had been a very light domestic comedy with a cricket background, but when Rattigan was tempted again into television with *Heart to Heart* (1962) he produced a major serious work for the occasion. Designed for an international series to which each country in Eurovision would contribute a play which would receive a dozen or more nearly simultaneous productions in almost as many languages, *Heart to Heart* fell somewhat between two stools, being over-long for television while shorter than the average full-length theatrical play. The central character is the permanent interviewer on a nightly television programme of unscripted encounters with the great and famous. He discovers evidence that his next important subject, the new Minister of Labour, is a crook. The problem is whether he should ask those damaging questions in front of the camera and try to expose him: for one thing, the programme would no doubt be cut off the air before he could get far enough, and for another he might not be able to make his charges stick, and so probably end his own career. The central part of the play, with its built-in will-he, won't-he suspense and its two excellent character-studies of the indecisive, hard-drinking interviewer and the wily, devious old minister, is strong and holding, but other parts of the play, particularly the scenes concerning the interviewer's unhappy marriage, are not developed enough to balance the main plot or be satisfactory in themselves, but at the same time bulk too large to work as a mere sub-plot. These faults of construction might be corrected in the stage version Rattigan announced he intended to write, but up to now it has not materialized.

Much of Rattigan's time at this period was taken up with film scripting, though there was nothing in *The V.I.P's* (1963) or *The Yellow Rolls Royce* (1964) which seemed to need his talents or show them distinctively at work. In *Man and Boy* (1963), however, he returned to the theatre with one of his finest plays, and a striking indication of his ability to use the form of the well-made drawing-room drama with the utmost ease and virtuosity to do exactly what he wants it to do. What he wants it to do in this case is rather curious. The play observes the unities to the letter: the action takes place entirely in the studio flat of Basil Anthony, illegitimate son of Gregor Antonescu, an internationally famous financier. His father, whose empire is crumbling, has gone to ground here to make a last desperate attempt to repair his fortunes and to come to terms with his son. The play follows the twists and turns of his fate during these last few hours, the central episode being that in which Antonescu sets out with all his old cunning to disarm a snobbish business rival whom he knows to be a homosexual by pretending that he is too and that his attractive son is a young and conceivably available lover. This, naturally, does not exactly help his attempts to make up with the young man, whose feelings towards him are pretty mixed even at the beginning. Nor does it manage, finally, to extract Antonescu from his difficulties: gradually everyone gangs up on him until in the end, cornered, he takes the only conclusive way out.

Evidently there is a connection between this play and *The Deep Blue Sea*: both are studies of desperation, both show their central characters on the verge of suicide, and Antonescu, like Hester, is in his way obsessed with an impossible ideal, in his case a world where everyone and everything must consent to be juggled by him, for his own entertainment and, incidentally, profit. But *Man and Boy* is a distinct advance on *The Deep Blue Sea*, in that the earlier play, excellent as it is on its own chosen level, does not go much further than its text; everything in it is explicit, clear, and its effects can be completely analysed and explained. *Man and Boy*, for all its neatness as a piece of plotting, goes beyond this: it has the fascination of a tale that is told, not precisely explicable, seeming to imply much more than it says. For unlike *The Deep Blue Sea* it does not actually say anything: or what it has to say escapes all neat, pat formulation. It is the character-portrait of a man without qualities, and Rattigan seems in it for the first time to be moving outside the neat, clear-cut world of the well-made play, where there is always an explanation hidden somewhere in a secret drawer, and into the shifting, indeterminate world of contemporary drama, which might take as its motto Gertrude Stein's supposed last words 'What is the answer . . .? Very well then, what is the question?' But still preserving the form of the well-made play: a curious and potentially explosive combination.

Since then Rattigan's only play has been another television piece, equally haunting: *Nelson: A Portrait in Miniature* (1966). Here the subject is Nelson not as the national hero, but as a private (or would-be private) man; and Lady Hamilton not as a love goddess but as an aging, thickening, over-ripe drinker to whom he is shackled all the more conclusively because they are not married. The whole action takes place in one difficult week-end, in which a young relation gets a sharp insight into the characters of all those involved, even the supposedly monstrous wife, against whom Nelson's only real reproach is that she has done the one unforgivable thing, forgiven him. Again Rattigan approaches the unknowable, but with less confidence than in *Ross*, where explanations are given without compunction. The explanations in *Nelson* are tentative, partial, and in consequence the effect is more believable and certainly more imaginatively compelling. The surface is as impeccably neat as ever, but clearly something dark and unmanageable is bubbling underneath.

Rattigan then remains in a paradoxical position. Though

accepted during the later 1950s and 1960s, the period of the 'New Drama', as quite simply the last unquestioning inheritor of the realistic tradition initiated by Robertson, he really has much more about him of the conscious revivalist: *The Winslow Boy* is a completely deliberate harking-back to the sort of drama Shaw set out to destroy, and it is only after this, his 'diploma piece' as it were, that Rattigan settles down in the post-war years, the years after all in which verse drama and fantasy were considered the hallmarks of the new theatre, to cultivating his own peculiar garden, a wilful and self-conscious neo-classicist. But this technical harking-back has not prevented him from moving forward, from using the new freedoms won by the new drama – to discuss homosexuality openly on stage, for instance – and from dispensing with the tendency to over-neatness, over-explicitness which marred many otherwise admirable plays in the heyday of the well-made drawing-room drama. *Man and Boy* and *Nelson* suggest that he may be moving towards a new synthesis of old and new, perhaps even a well-made play, 1960s model. And it may not, after all, be before time.

The way we live now

If Terence Rattigan's return to the well-made domestic drama in all its late nineteenth-century splendour with *The Winslow Boy* was something in the nature of a deliberate, self-conscious revival, it would seem to have been premature. When it appeared in 1946 the last notable play in its genre was Galsworthy's *Loyalties*, twenty-four years earlier. During that time well-made comedy had flourished and adapted itself successfully to a changed theatre; Rattigan himself had contributed to the later stages of this process. And drawing-room dramas of a sort remained a staple commodity of the popular stage, though seldom particularly distinguished in their craftsmanship or greeted with much critical enthusiasm.

Opinion was agreed, in fact, that something new was needed to revitalize serious British drama. And since T. S. Eliot's *Murder in the Cathedral* (1935) the idea had been gaining currency that that something might be verse. Just at the time that *The Winslow Boy* came out it suddenly seemed that everybody was writing verse plays. Seasons of them were given in London, and one of them, Ronald Duncan's *This Way to the Tomb*, had quite a vogue in 1946. So did a one-act verse comedy by Christopher Fry, *A Phoenix too Frequent*, and two years later he consolidated his reputation with a major commercial success, *The Lady's Not For Burning*. Theatricalism was in vogue: the bubbling poetry of Fry, rendered volubly inarticulate at the wonder of merely being alive, the flash and outbreak of Anouilh's early plays, which only in the late 1940s and early 1950s found their way into English theatres.

But this particular fair summer of fancy quickly drooped, and critics and public were again ready to decry the English theatre as moribund – despite Terence Rattigan – when in May 1956 came *Look Back in Anger*. No need to rehearse again the brilliant history of British drama in the next decade. John Osborne's impassioned monologue plays; the intense, finely chiselled works of Harold Pinter; the rough, well-meaning social dramas of Arnold Wesker; the obsessive, loose-jointed farces of Henry Livings; the intellectual teasings of N. F. Simpson; the voluble, extravagant tragi-comedies of John Arden; the patterns of sounds and actions elaborated by Ann Jellicoe; the director's field-days Joan Littlewood had with Brendan Behan and Shelagh Delaney. It has been rich, strange, infinitely various, and little or none of it has had anything conceivable to do with the dead and buried well-made play.

Or has it? Let us not squabble over what exactly we mean by well-made. Of course many of these plays are extremely well made; formally they work, they satisfy, according to their own inherent standards. But those standards are not those of Pinero either in construction or in concern for surface verisimilitude. Arnold Wesker may aim at untampered realism in his dialogue (whether he achieves it is another matter), but he has no noticeable care for form at all. Henry Livings has a clear and consistent view of form, based on his own system of ten-minute sequences corresponding with what he estimates as the ten-minute attention-span of the ordinary audience. It works, but it would make Sardou turn in his grave. And so on. Nearly all the writers in the New British drama are just not interested in any of the concerns which were paramount in British drama on and off for nearly a hundred years, from Robertson to Rattigan. If they seem to be, like Peter Shaffer in *Five Finger Exercise*, they are likely to be dismissed as old fashioned for their pains; if they apply the old techniques to the new subject-matter, like Joe Orton in *Entertaining Mr Sloane*, they may be denounced as 'commercial'.

And yet all is not quite so simple as it seems. For one thing, there is always the possibility that if the old-fashioned well-made drama is really dead and gone a brand new, 1960s sort is just round the corner: one which accepts the continuing validity of certain basic prerequisites in the sort of play-making advocated by Archer, while radically modifying the way in which they are applied. Consider, for example, the plays of Harold Pinter in this light. What else is *The Birthday Party* but a well-made drawing-room drama complete in every detail, even down to the meticulously realistic dialogue, except that the exposition is left out altogether? It would be easy to write in the necessary explanations: how Stanley came to be living in this seaside boarding house, what his secret is and why McCann and Goldberg came to get him. But of course this is not what the play is about: it is the process that interests Pinter, the series of happenings, and not the precise whys and wherefores. These are totally incoherent, as necessarily they have to be in so much of life, where no explanations are offered and we must make the best we can of it.

If Pinter suggests one way of using the virtues of the well-made tradition in a specifically modern way, John Arden suggests another. We tend to forget nowadays that one of the essential ingredients of the well-made play, from Scribe to Somerset Maugham, was lots of plot. Noël Coward put a stop to that, but before him the great test of a dramatist's skill in this tradition was his ability to handle plot, to put over all the necessary preliminary information and then to articulate a long and involved series of interesting interrelated happenings. Now hardly any recent British dramatist, whatever his other allegiances, is willing to show any interest in plot *per se*.

Except John Arden. And the trouble he has had up to now in achieving any widespread public acceptance is, I suspect, largely the result of his passion for plot in operatic profusion. A play like *The Workhouse Donkey*, with its innumerable characters and endless twists and turns as everyone schemes against everyone else in a grand free-for-all of municipal corruption, would not have presented any fundamental difficulty to a theatre-goer of the 1890s, though he would have found the idiom unsettling and thought the play more than a little untidy. In any case, the play has just about everything Scribe, in simpler days, would have looked for in a *pièce bien faite*: a thrill a minute and no time for the audience to stop and catch their breath. But modern audiences, inured to plays with little plot or none at all, do not have the stamina or the training.

And yet, can it be that plot is coming back into favour, that the conventions of craftsmanlike construction are again giving pleasure in themselves? The vogue in 1965–67 for Wilde, Maugham, Pinero, Coward, Lonsdale, and even Harley Granville Barker and Henry Arthur Jones, must mean something. Of course it might just be an urge to escape into a past which seems relatively carefree, or a desire to hear highly literate talk in the theatre again – after all Ben Travers and G.B.S. were equally appreciated in the same period. But there seems to be something more to it than that. Even escapism must always be escape in some particular direction, in search of some particular elusive thing desired.

The revival of the well-made plays of the past today may suggest that the wheel has come full circle, and that audiences are ready at last, having got the poison of Shavian puritanism out of their system, to enjoy again sophisticated dramatic entertainment for what it is instead of cursing it in the name of what perhaps it ought to be. At any rate it demonstrates a hunger in audiences today for something a lot of modern drama is not giving it, a chance to be diverted intelligently without being willy-nilly involved. Pinter certainly does this – his plays exist immaculately in a world of their own, self-defining and self-sufficient, to tell audiences a story and leave it at that. One or two of the other dramatists of the last ten years approach this condition, on and off – John Arden, Henry Livings. But in general the want which clearly exists is ignored.

How long can it remain so? The problem may be vital if popular entertainment and seriously intentioned drama are not to lose touch altogether in the modern theatre. And perhaps even the most serious critics may be growing more willing to accept the value of old-fashioned story-telling technique as at least one quality in the theatre, one of many. Towards the end of 1966 I took part in a symposium on 'The New Drama – Whither?' or some such subject at a theatre club meeting of advanced inclinations. The others involved were an avant-garde playwright and a director of one of our major subsidized companies. During the discussion a lady in the audience announced that she represented the philistine spectator who just wanted a good laugh, a good cry and either way a good story in the theatre: she berated us for not caring about the needs of such people, and clearly did not believe our protestations that we did, very much. But when the audience had gone and the speakers were relaxing over a cup of tea conversation turned to what had first got us excited by the theatre: *A Streetcar Named Desire*, volunteered one, *Ring Round the Moon* ventured another. There was an appreciative pause. Another piped up. '*The Deep Blue Sea* – now *there* was a play for you . . .'

Notes on sources

These are the sources for quotations in the text, identified by the first words.

Page

94. IT IS NOT QUITE . . . *Sunday Times and Special,* October 27 1907
100. THESE PLAYS . . . *The Summing Up,* p. 119
103. THE DRAMA I SAW . . . *Collected Plays* III, pp. xvi–xvii
108. I GREW CONSCIOUS . . . *Collected Plays* III, p. xvii
114. DO YOU REALIZE . . . *The Life and Letters of Henry Arthur Jones,* p. 411
127. IN HIS CONSTRUCTION . . . Introduction to *Bittersweet and Other Plays,* reprinted in *Theatrical Companion to Maugham,* pp. 144–147
128. IT IS IN HIS DIALOGUE . . . ibid.
134. THE DERNIER CRI . . . *Sunday Times,* November 30 1924
138. FROM THE 'EIGHTIES . . . *Play Parade* II (1950 edition), pp. viii–x
142. AMUSING NO DOUBT . . . *World Drama,* p. 839

Bibliographical Note

All the plays I discuss have been published at some time; very few by the dramatists before Maugham are conveniently in print now. These are the best editions, and such of the various books on the dramatists and on the dramatic history of the period as seem to me of lasting use today.

ROBERTSON

Principal Dramatic Works of Thomas William Robertson. Two vols. Sampson Low, Marston, Searle and Rivington. 1889

T. EDGAR PEMBERTON: *The Life and Writings of T. W. Robertson.* Richard Bentley and Son. 1893

MAYNARD SAVIN: *Thomas William Robertson: His Plays and Stagecraft.* Brown University, Providence R.I. 1950

THE 1870S

ALLARDYCE NICOLL: *A History of Late XIXth Century Drama, 1850–1900.* Two vols. Cambridge University Press. 1946

GEORGE ROWELL: *The Victorian Theatre: A Survey.* Oxford University Press. 1956

SIR ARTHUR PINERO: 'The Theatre in the 'Seventies'. In *The Eighteen-Seventies.* Ed. H. Granville-Barker. Cambridge University Press. 1929

HENRY ARTHUR JONES

Representative Plays by Henry Arthur Jones. Four vols. Macmillan. 1925

The Renascence of the English Drama. Macmillan. 1895

The Theatre of Ideas. Chapman and Hall. 1915

BIBLIOGRAPHICAL NOTE

DORIS ARTHUR JONES: *The Life and Letters of Henry Arthur Jones.* Gollancz. 1930

ARTHUR WING PINERO

The Plays of Arthur W. Pinero. Separate volumes. Heinemann. 1893–

W. HAMILTON FYFE: *Sir Arthur Pinero's Plays and Players.* Benn. 1930

W. D. DUNKEL: *Sir Arthur Pinero.* Chicago. 1941

THE 1890s

GEORGE BERNARD SHAW: *Our Theatres in the Nineties.* Three vols. Constable. 1932

H. GRANVILLE-BARKER: 'The Coming of Ibsen'. In *The Eighteen Eighties.* Ed. Walter de la Mare. Cambridge University Press. 1930

WILLIAM ARCHER: *Play-Making.* Chapman and Hall. 1912

OSCAR WILDE: *Plays.* Penguin Books. 1954

MARTIN MEISEL: *Shaw and the Nineteenth-Century Theatre.* Oxford University Press. 1963

W. SOMERSET MAUGHAN

Collected Plays. Three Vols. Heinemann. 1952

The Summing Up. Collected Edition. Heinemann. 1948

RAYMOND MANDER and JOE MITCHENSON: *Theatrical Companion to Maugham.* Rockliff. 1955

BARKER, GALSWORTHY, LONSDALE

HANKIN: *Dramatic Works.* Three vols. Martin Secker, 1912

GALSWORTHY: *Plays.* Duckworth. 1929

GRANVILLE-BARKER: *Three Plays.* Sidgwick and Jackson. 1909
The Madras House. Sidgwick and Jackson. 1911

C. B. PURDOM: *Harley Granville-Barker.* Rockliff. 1955

LONSDALE: Uniform edition in separate vols. Collins. 1923–

FRANCES DONALDSON: *Freddy Lonsdale.* Heinemann. 1957

THE WELL-MADE PLAY

NOËL COWARD

Play Parade. Six vols to date. Heinemann. 1934–
Suite in Three Keys. Heinemann. 1966
Present Indicative. Heinemann. 1937
Future Indefinite. Heinemann. 1945
RAYMOND MANDER and JOE MITCHENSON: *Theatrical Companion to Coward.* Rockliff. 1957

TERENCE RATTIGAN

Collected Plays. Three vols to date. Hamish Hamilton. 1953–
Man and Boy. Hamish Hamilton. 1964

Index

171

DRAMABOOKS

WHEN ORDERING, please use the Standard Book Number consisting of the publisher's prefix, 8090-, plus the five digits following each title. (Note that the numbers given in this list are for paperback editions only. Many of the books are also available in cloth.)

Shakespeare and the Elizabethans by Henri Fluchère (0501-8)
On Dramatic Method by Harley Granville-Barker (0502-6)
George Bernard Shaw by G. K. Chesterton (0503-4)
Paradox of Acting by Diderot and *Masks or Faces?* by William Archer (0504-0)
The Scenic Art by Henry James (0505-0)
Hazlitt on Theatre ed. by William Archer and Robert Lowe (0507-9)
The Fervent Years by Harold Clurman (0508-5)
The Quintessence of Ibsenism by Bernard Shaw (0509-3)
Papers on Playmaking ed. by Brander Matthews (0510-7)
Papers on Acting ed. by Brander Matthews (0511-5)
The Theatre by Stark Young (0512-3)
Immortal Shadows by Stark Young (0513-1)
Shakespeare: A Survey by E. K. Chambers (0514-X)
The English Drama Critics ed. by James Agate (0515-8)
Japanese Theatre by Faubion Bowers (0516-6)
Shaw's Dramatic Criticism (1895–98) ed. by John F. Matthews (0517-4)
Shaw on Theatre ed. by E. J. West (0518-2)
The Book of Job as a Greek Tragedy by Horace Meyer Kallen (0519-0)
Molière: The Man Seen Through the Plays by Ramon Fernandez (0520-4)
Greek Tragedy by Gilbert Norwood (0521-2)
Samuel Johnson on Shakespeare ed. by W. K. Wimsatt, Jr. (0522-0)
The Poet in the Theatre by Ronald Peacock (0523-9)
Chekhov the Dramatist by David Magarshack (0524-7)
Theory and Technique of Playwriting by John Howard Lawson (0525-5)
The Art of the Theatre by Henri Ghéon (0526-3)
Aristotle's Poetics with an Introduction by Francis Fergusson (0527-1)
The Origin of the Theater by Benjamin Hunningher (0528-X)
Playwrights on Playwriting by Toby Cole (0529-8)
The Sense of Shakespeare's Sonnets by Edward Hubler (0530-1)
The Development of Shakespeare's Imagery by Wolfgang Clemen (0531-X)
Stanislavsky on the Art of the Stage trans. by David Magarshack (0532-8)
Metatheatre: A New View of Dramatic Form by Lionel Abel (0533-6)
The Seven Ages of the Theatre by Richard Southern (0534-4)
The Death of Tragedy by George Steiner (0535-2)
Greek Comedy by Gilbert Norwood (0536-0)
Ibsen: Letters and Speeches ed. by Evert Sprinchorn (0537-9)
The Testament of Samuel Beckett by J. Jacobsen and W. R. Mueller (0538-7)
On Racine by Roland Barthes (0539-5)
American Playwrights on Drama ed. by Horst Frenz (0540-9)
How Shakespeare Spent the Day by Ivor Brown (0541-7)
Brecht on Theatre ed. by John Willett (0542-5)
Costume in the Theatre by James Laver (0543-3)
Ionesco and Genet by J. Jacobsen and W. R. Mueller (0544-1)
Commedia dell'Arte by Giacomo Oreglia (0545-X)

For a complete list of plays (including the New Mermaids and Spotlight Dramabooks series), please write to Hill and Wang, 72 Fifth Avenue, New York, New York 10011.